W9-BVJ-836

Praise for
Going All the Way

"Craig's practical book should be a mandatory read for anyone who wants to be happily married someday."

—SHAUNTI FELDHAHN, nationally syndicated columnist and best-selling author of *For Women Only*

"*Going All the Way* clearly illustrates how Jesus Christ is truly the center of every enduring and endearing marriage."

—PASTOR MARK DRISCOLL, founder of Mars Hill Church, Seattle

"*Going All the Way* is a great resource for anyone in our generation who wants to build a relationship that will go the distance like God intended."

—MARGARET FEINBERG, speaker and author of *The Organic God* and *God Whispers*

"*Going All the Way* has the potential to not only change the way you view marriage, but also the way our culture treats it."

—ED YOUNG, SENIOR PASTOR, Fellowship Church, and author of *The Creative Marriage*

"With wit and wisdom, Craig will guide you into a gold mine of relational riches."

—SHANNON ETHRIDGE, best-selling author of the Every Woman's Battle series and *Completely His*

"Craig shares real-life advice that is practical and biblically based, preparing you for a marriage that will not just survive, but thrive."

—RICK WARREN, Pastor of Saddleback Church and author of *The Purpose Driven Life*

"Craig Groeschel says it like it is. You'll be challenged and encouraged by his honesty and humor."

—MARK BATTERSON, Lead Pastor, National Community Church, and author of *In a Pit with a Lion on a Snowy Day*

"Craig Groeschel is a visionary… His leadership capacity has barely been tapped."

—DR. SAMUEL R. CHAND, author of *Failure: The Womb of Success* and *Futuring: Leading Your Church into Tomorrow*

"Craig Groeschel truly goes *all the way*—he digs deep, posing the questions we all have but are afraid to ask, and then answers them—with profound wisdom."

—BISHOP EDDIE L. LONG, Senior Pastor, New Birth Missionary Baptist Church and author of *It's Your Time*

"Craig boldly dives into our culture's many illusions of love and discovers what real love is."

—DAVE GIBBONS, Lead Pastor of NewSong

"Craig is a man who practices what he preaches. I am always excited to pick up his latest book."

—CRAIG GROSS, founder of xxxchurch.com

"Craig fully understands our generation's struggles and fears about making love last and provides practical, hope-filled guidance for imperfect people."

—JOHN BURKE, pastor and author of *No Perfect People Allowed*

GOING ALL THE WAY

CRAIG GROESCHEL

GOING ALL THE WAY

preparing for a marriage that goes the distance

MULTNOMAH
BOOKS

Going All the Way
Published by Multnomah Books
12265 Oracle Boulevard, Suite 200
Colorado Springs, Colorado 80921
A division of Random House Inc.

Italics in Scripture quotations indicate the author's added emphasis.

Details and names in some anecdotes and stories have been changed with permission to protect the identities of the persons involved.

ISBN 978-1-59052-938-6

Library of Congress Cataloging-in-Publication Data
Groeschel, Craig.
Going all the way / Craig Groeschel.—1st ed.
p. cm.
ISBN-13: 978-1-59052-938-6
1. Mate selection—Religious aspects—Christianity. 2. Marriage—Religious aspects—Christianity. 3. Sex—Religious aspects—Christianity. 4. Man-woman relationships—Religious aspects—Christianity. I. Title.
BV835.G745 2007
241'.6765—dc22

2007021486

Printed in the United States of America
2007—First Edition

10 9 8 7 6 5 4 3 2 1

CONTENTS

1

DESIGNED TO GO ALL THE WAY

Is she the one? Four words that shaped my hope. My wish. My prayer.

Her name was Kelli. She was more beautiful than words could describe. Her tan was perfectly golden. Her blond hair could've starred in any shampoo commercial. Her smile stopped me in my tracks. And her legs… I'll just say, praise God for legs!

Kelli was wildly popular, completely feminine, yet also athletic. Confident, yet humble. Exciting, yet pure. Every guy I knew liked her.

I *loved* her.

Kelli dominated my thought life. *Will she go out with me? Go with me? MARRY ME? Have my children? Live with me in a house with a white picket fence? You know, for our dog. Not a chick dog, like a Shih Tzu. A real dog. Maybe a black Lab. Or a German shepherd. Named Joe...*

In my daydreams I was always the hero, rescuing Kelli from attackers using my finely honed nun-chucks skills. I protected her while stranded on a desert island. I kept her warm during a dangerous blizzard. All my fantasies ended the same: Kelli fell in love with me, then kissed me until I couldn't breathe. It was our destiny to be together. Forever. (Can you hear a Luther Vandross love song playing softly?)

Maybe my imagination was getting ahead of me. After all, she'd never spoken to me. She didn't even know my name. And, well, we were both in seventh grade.

But trifling details couldn't weaken her magnetic pull. My life orbited around her. The mounting pressure seemed too much for my heart to bear.

Could she be "*the one*"?

On the Way to One

You're probably not in the seventh grade (and glad you never have to return to junior high hell again). But that longing for *the one* is virtually universal. You've yearned for the one to be part of your life—your soul mate, bound by passionate affection and a forever vow.

Does a fulfilling, lifelong commitment exist in your future?

You hope so, but maybe you're not sure. When someone cute moves to your school or starts a new job at your office, you wonder, *Could this be the one?*

Or maybe you're already in love with someone. At this moment all the love songs on the radio make sense. You spend hours in the Hallmark store choosing the perfect card for your honey-pie-love-bunches. (You leave with eleven cards and a stuffed walrus.) For you the question isn't in the back of your mind; it's front and center, and you believe you know the answer. *I think there's* a one *for me after all!*

But perhaps you're on the other side of the relationship divide, and you're not so optimistic at the moment. You're recovering from a painful breakup. Disillusioned. You were sure you'd met the one. But that was before the lying. Before the drifting apart. Before the restraining order. Before the dude like Jim Carrey's character in *The Cable Guy.*

Maybe you were married. With all your heart, you believed it was forever, but it simply wasn't true.

Whether it was divorce or a breakup, you feel alone. You ache, wondering when the pain will ease, if you'll ever love again. Were you even meant to find the one? Does *wanting* it to be true *make* it true?

I don't blame you. I've felt the same way. Slightly optimistic one moment, devastatingly depressed and hopeless the next.

I always hated the person with all the answers. You know, the married friend who preaches, "You just have to not care.

Then you'll find the one." Or "If you just surrender, the perfect person will show up."

Whatever.

You might be thinking that *I'm* the annoying know-it-all right now. *What does some married pastor-guy know? What could I gain from reading another stupid book about preparing for marriage?*

Good questions. I'll admit, I don't have surefire formulas for "how to find the love of your life in thirty days or less." I won't try to sell you on "five steps to living happily ever after." My goal is twofold. First, I'll offer a different perspective on a marriage that lasts a lifetime. And second, I plan to offer you…

Hope.

Reservations for One

It's hard to be hopeful these days, to be confident you'll find your soul mate and enjoy a long and fulfilling life together. Many twenty- and thirty-somethings today see marriage as a risky venture. They're not cynical, just observant. They see plenty of unhappy couples, dismal divorce statistics, and heartbreak in families, often their own.

No wonder people are getting married later in life, with more reservations and less success. Many are hiding from their fears by building their careers, postponing marriage indefinitely.

Others keep searching. That's what I did. Though I wanted to do what was right, the Bible seemed like a distant, out-of-touch rule book. You might relate. People say: "Sleep around.

Focus on externals. Splurge on your toys. Don't worry about consequences. The future's uncertain. Live for today. Why risk missing out? Don't let religion hold you back. You deserve to get what you want now…"

This approach to relationships has become the new normal. Problem is, the new normal doesn't work. (Have you noticed?) In fact, it leads to a lot of needless suffering, injury, and disillusionment.

I wrote this book because people in my generation are making decisions way before marriage that actually sabotage what they really want for their futures. We don't make these decisions in a vacuum, or because we're the biggest losers ever to walk the planet. We make them in large part because our culture constantly bombards us with deeply flawed ideas about what it means to be in love, to be happy, to be sexual, to have a meaningful relationship with a person of the opposite sex…and we buy the lies. Many people I meet—sadly, even many Christians—have little or no idea that a better way exists. Frankly, I'm tired of waiting for premarital counseling to lay out a biblical plan for finding lasting intimacy in marriage. By then, for many, it's just too late. Too late to prevent a lot of hurt. Too late to prevent the death of a dream.

But it doesn't have to be that way.

All the Way, Not Partway

If God has a marriage planned for you, think about this: *you have already been created to "go all the way."*

When I say "go all the way," I'm not talking about the "I Wanna Sex You Up," people-disposable games many settle for. I'm not talking about taking what you want sexually (or giving away sexually what someone else demands) in a relationship before marriage. Instead, I'm affirming God's plan for a marriage that goes all the way in sexual, emotional, and spiritual fulfillment. And that goes all the way through the years and decades of your life.

Most people, Christ followers or not, deeply desire exactly this. But a closer look at how many of us pursue this goal before and after marriage shows that, while our desires are normal, our methods are routinely misguided. Turns out, how we set about to go *all the way* in our most important human relationship takes us only *partway.*

So what do you do when you want a marriage that soars in a world where most crash before takeoff? What do you do when you have a dream for intimacy, but most married couples you know are strangers to each other? What do you do when you desire a marriage that goes all the way?

I propose that you do something different.

In this book, I'm going to show you that your desire for lifelong intimacy is a God-given desire. And I'm going to help you prepare for that relationship. But we're not going to travel the typical path. Ours will be delightfully different. Oddly godly. I won't try to fool you—a good marriage is never easy. But it *is* absolutely possible.

If you haven't traveled the sinful road, laced with land mines,

I hope to help you stay off that path. And if you've already taken some hits, we'll be able to relate and then begin to identify a God-blessed way forward. Together we'll plan for your relational success, examining how to conduct your relationships in a positive, fulfilling way. I'll offer ideas about what to do and what *not* to do. You'll learn to prepare for a marriage that goes all the way to God's best. A marriage that doesn't just survive, but thrives.

Let me warn you: this book may require a radical shift in your thinking. If small changes would do the trick, everyone would be making them. Minor adjustments produce marginal results. Most of us need to overhaul our thought processes. To experience the kind of relationships we long for, we must, with God's help, prepare to be genuinely different.

We have to redefine and choose to aim for a new kind of "normal." Because the current one doesn't deliver.

Of course, not everyone wants to get married. And not every one who wants to marry *will* marry. I also know that some people do nearly everything wrong yet end up in wonderful marriages. And that some others do everything possible to find their spouses while honoring biblical guidelines and *still* end up in miserable relationships.

Hey, it's a crazy world. What can I say?

So I can't make guarantees. But I will present some powerful, time-tested principles based on God's Word. His Word is true and constant, like the law of gravity is true and constant. We ignore either at our own risk. Consider what the law of gravity suggests about how to get off your roof: you may not break a leg (or worse) *every* time you choose to jump, but the law of gravity definitely argues for using a ladder. Similarly, my starting point for *Going All the Way* is the Bible. Because we have been created by a loving, intentional God, we're wise to consider the relational laws He has put in place. When we don't follow the path He lays out in Scripture, we're inviting injury to ourselves and others. But thankfully, the opposite is also true: when we *do* follow the path of truth, we're far more likely to discover and enjoy the marriage we hope for and that God desires for us.

Good-Bye, Kelli

In case you're wondering, my seventh-grade dream girl, Kelli, wasn't the one. (I told myself it was her loss.) After a bunch of wasted years, several misfires, some relational train wrecks, and a couple of broken hearts, I was ready to write off all hope for a great marriage. *No one is faithful,* I thought. *Almost all marriages I know stink. Why bother?*

Then I met a girl named Amy, and God blessed our friendship. It took time for my battered heart to fully trust her—or even trust myself. But with God's help and encouragement from friends, Amy and I grew together.

We didn't "go all the way" by the world's definition. We wanted something more. We wanted to go all the way in truth and love. We wanted God's normal.

Seventeen years and six children later, I'm honored to tell you that you can have hope for a great marriage. (Yes, you read that right. We have six kids. What can I say? Amy can't keep her hands off me. What? You don't buy that?)

No matter what you've seen, how badly you've been hurt, or how afraid you are, with God, a lasting and intimate marriage is possible.

Even in a world where happy marriages are often considered just another fairy tale, it can be real for you. If you want something few have—genuine closeness, trust, respect, and lasting commitment—you'll have to do what few do.

Go all the way, God's way.

In the pages ahead, we'll find out what that really means.

2

FINDING THE ONE

Melissa sat staring at her Bible, hoping to find comfort but unable to make out the words through her tears. Her heart was broken. Again.

How did it happen? How could I be so stupid?

Cody had seemed so perfect. He was charming, funny, downright cute. Most of all, he was encouraging—always lifting Melissa's spirits.

All signals were positive. He took her to church. Paid for their dates (and never burped out loud). Treated her gently. Took her to meet his parents.

Melissa tried to move slowly, prayerfully, cautiously. All the while hoping, dreaming, wondering, *Could Cody be the one?*

Five weeks into the relationship he actually said the three big words: *I love you.* Melissa's heart melted.

Melissa loved him too. On that night, thirty-seven days after they met, Melissa gave him her whole body—in love—convinced he was *the one.*

The next day she regretted it. Deeply. It wasn't that she was a virgin. She'd already given herself to three other guys. But she'd hoped to wait until marriage with her *one.* She tried to explain that they shouldn't keep having sex, but Cody didn't understand. So the sex continued. And so did her guilt.

Four months later he dumped her.

Where did it go wrong? Why didn't I see it coming? Melissa couldn't figure it out. Maybe she was just destined to hurt.

Have you tried the traditional formula, hoping to meet *the one*? You kept your antennae continuously alert for that someone at the gym, at church, in the grocery store by the frozen tamales. Perhaps you took the more aggressive approach—Internet dating, speed dating, or—*gasp!*—blind dating. ("She's got a great personality. Really.")

Why do we subject ourselves to such craziness?

Looking-for-*the-one* dating.

Oops-look-what-I've-done dating.

Hit-and-run dating.

I'll-never-be-a-nun dating.

Attila-the-Hun dating. (I'm not sure what this means, but I got on a roll and couldn't stop.)

We do it out of desperation. Because deep down, engraved in the DNA of our hearts, most of us believe, really believe... *that we'll never be fulfilled in life until we meet "the one."*

Guess what? It's true. You can't be fulfilled until you meet *the one.* Without *the one,* you'll always be slightly, or not so slightly, empty. Without *the one,* you'll always know there's something more, something important you just can't seem to find. Something inside cries for deep acceptance, shared intimacy, unbreakable commitment. Somehow you know that to be complete, to feel whole you have to meet *the one.*

But who is that one? And when and where will you ever meet?

The Quest for One-derful

After Kelli, the seventh-grade girl with the killer legs, rejected me, I met Jana in chemistry class. The collar on her polo shirt was flipped up just so. (A sign from God? This *was* the eighties.) And the way she dissected a frog—amazing. Could she be *the one*? One day I put it all on the line and approached her.

Smile, I told myself. *Don't drool.* Hands sweating, heart pounding, I cautiously moved in.

On the inside my nerves were redlining with an intoxicating mix of excitement, adrenaline, and panic. On the outside, a calm, cool Johnny Depp took over.

"Hi," I said bravely. *Good so far.* The first word is always the toughest. *Gulp.* "M-my name is Craig Groeschel." *Keep breathing.* "Wanna go to a movie sometime?"

I know. Not the smoothest approach. But it was the best line in my verbal arsenal at the time.

Jana looked at me, gently touched her raised collar, and said, "I'll meet you tonight at the 7:05 show."

TOUCHDOWN! HOME RUN!

VICTORY!

Over the next several hours, I tried on different outfits. With an extra squirt of cologne and my favorite Izod shirt tucked neatly into my best butt-gripping jeans, I met Jana by the ticket booth. Life couldn't have been better.

Or so I thought.

Everything was going as planned until one fatal error in judgment. I was so mesmerized by Jana that when we sat down, I forgot to immediately slide my arm around the back of her chair, giving me complete access to her shoulder.

Idiot!

If I wanted to salvage the date, I was left with no choice but to fall back on the old fake-yawn-and-stretch technique. *I'm gonna do this,* I promised myself. I mustered my courage. *One... Don't back out... Two... Here goes... Three!*

I drew the deepest, yawniest breath I could fake and swiftly lifted my right arm.

That's when I made my second big mistake. My elbow

smacked Jana square on the nose. In horrifying slow motion, I watched the whiplash action of her head flinging backward.

This was bad.

Blood trickled from her nose. But, as they say, every nose bloodied by a high-school klutz opens a door of opportunity. I grabbed my napkin and leaned over to comfort my dream girl. I tried again to put my arm around her. She reflexively jerked away. "Why don't we just hold hands?" she said.

Sure, it was a consolation prize. But I gladly accepted. How could I possibly mess that up?

Mistake number three.

I accidentally wedged two fingers between her middle finger and ring finger, creating the most awkward handholding experience in history. Did I have the courage to simply adjust my fingers? No. Afraid of any sudden movements, I sat through the rest of the movie that way, our hands awkwardly intertwined like a deformed pretzel.

There was no second date. She said—I'm not making this up—that I was like Richie Cunningham, and she wanted the Fonz.

That still hurts.

Will the Real Dreamer Please Stand Up?

Why do we subject ourselves to such pain? Are we crazy? Do we think the best we can do is roll the relational dice, hoping to hit the marriage jackpot?

Or do we believe a marriage that goes all the way—blessed by God—is actually possible and is worth any risk necessary to achieve it?

For as long as I can remember, I dreamed of having a great marriage. What could be better than sharing each day with your best friend, then at night getting naked together? I hoped to one day build a home, then a family, then a lifetime of memories with my spouse. I envisioned sharing secrets known only to us, holding hands, taking long walks. I imagined having our first child, a son. I'd watch him take his first steps and ride his bike. I envisioned him protecting our second child, his little sister, the joy of our hearts.

I pictured us in church. On vacations. At Sunday afternoon picnics in the park. We'd grow old together, play with grandkids, take up competitive dominoes in the nursing home, and leave a legacy of love that had grown with each passing day.

Was that too much to hope for? If God wanted it for me—and I was sure He did—then it must come true (maybe not the dominoes part).

Looking back, I see that my deepest desires were *not* too much to hope for. They had been planted in me by God. So what I longed for was right and good. But some of my operating assumptions were definitely wrong. Little things, like getting the timing right. (Finding my soul mate at thirteen? Not likely!) And big things, like putting my life together in the right order.

Let me try to explain.

First Things First

Order matters. In some aspects of life, the right order makes all the difference in the world.

For example, most men will tell you that the proper way to finish a shower is to get out, look admiringly at yourself in the mirror, and drip-dry.

And everyone who's anyone first applies deodorant, then gets dressed (thus avoiding the get-dressed-first-then-lift-up-your-shirt deodorant streak down the side of your clothes).

How about shoes and socks? It's always sock, sock, then shoe, shoe. (If you get dressed sock, shoe, sock, shoe, I can give you the name of a good counselor.)

And, of course, when going to the movies and choosing between (a) getting your seats first (so you can sit in the middle and hopefully not have to share the armrest with a stranger), then sending someone out for popcorn and soft drinks; or (b) the life-is-short, get-the-refreshments-first approach...*(drum-roll)*...actually, both are wrong. Don't buy those overpriced refreshments. Just smuggle in your own.

Okay, so order doesn't always matter. But when it comes to God, *it matters.* Doing some things in the right order is essential for spiritual success—and, therefore, for every other kind of success. How do I know? Jesus said so.

A religious leader once asked Jesus, "Teacher, which is the greatest commandment in the Law?"

Jesus replied, "'Love the Lord your God with all your heart and with all your soul and with all your mind.' This is the first and greatest commandment. And the second is like it: 'Love your neighbor as yourself'" (Matthew 22:36–39).

Jesus's reply forever reminds us of the priority most of us forget. And He confronts and turns upside down the world's accepted sense of order. *Loving the Lord is our first priority.* Before anything else, Jesus wants to be first. Without Jesus in first place, what comes next will never quite work, including our love relationships. So if you're looking for the one, desiring more than anything else to one day meet your one, embrace this:

Jesus is *the One.*

He's the person you should reach out to with all your heart *first.* He's the One who will complete your soul.

When I say, "Jesus is the One," I'm not just throwing a preacher's platitude at you. Loving the Lord *first* is a practical principle for getting the most out of life. Only when the Lord is in His rightful place can we move beyond the first and greatest commandment and start successfully living out the second priority—loving someone else. Like a spouse. When we learn to love *Him* with all our hearts, we start to understand love. We love only because He first loved us (see 1 John 4:19). Without experiencing the purity of a love relationship with God, we can't share that same kind of love with another person.

Notice the wording of the second commandment: "Love

your neighbor *as yourself*." The implication: you can't love someone else—even your life partner—unless you love yourself. How do you learn to love yourself in the healthy, biblical sense? You enter into a love relationship with the God of the universe, with the Jesus of the cross.

Then you begin to understand what you're really worth to the One who dreamed you up in eternity past and skillfully crafted you in your mother's womb. You see more and more clearly His love for you. And you begin to think and feel in accordance with His thoughts and feelings. You start to love yourself in a godly, healthy way...and then you're able to *really* love others.

Most people don't love themselves. Do you? Be honest. For years I didn't even like myself, much less *love* myself. Outwardly I appeared to have it together, but inwardly I was falling apart.

I spent a lot of time searching for *the one*—in my mind, a woman who'd complete me and make me happy. I thought I needed her because only she could make me feel good about myself. But I was looking for the wrong *one*. And until I found the real *One*, I was unable to give away true, lasting love because I didn't know God's love.

Are you ready for a radical thought? Don't miss it. *You can't know the intimate marriage you desire...until you know Jesus first.*

You have to receive *His* love before you can give it. His love must overtake you, envelop you, and fill you. Only then can you share it with another.

WHOLEHEARTED DEVOTION TO YOUR *ONE*

When you put Jesus first in your life, people tend to make fun of you. You likely don't fit in with the "hot" crowd. You probably spend your time much differently than most, pursuing God passionately in all you do. You don't live for the temporary material pleasures of this world. You have exceptionally high morals in a casually immoral world. You love those who don't know Christ. You care deeply about the poor. You're generous, giving away large portions of your income to support your church and other important causes. You aren't entertained by the same sinful images that mesmerize so many. You're distinctly different.

I'm not saying you're perfect. Neither would you. You've experienced your share of failures. You have your own little quirks that get on some people's nerves. You certainly won't hit the mark every time. But your standards are different. Your target is higher. And you hit it more often than not. You're not perfect, but you are being perfected.

You're a devoted follower of Christ...living for an audience of *One.*

If your heart is fully devoted to the One who gave it all for you, praise God! You're not of this world. You're an alien. A stranger. A friend of the Lord. Congratulations. You're on the narrow road, traveling with a few, on the path to maximum eternal fulfillment.

You're also, by the way, the perfect candidate for a great marriage.

So if you've placed your faith in Christ and met the One—whether five minutes ago or fifty years ago—it's important to *keep* Him in the number-one priority slot in your life from this point on. Because it's easy to let other people or things take His rightful place.

Jesus said in Matthew 6:33, "Seek first [God's] kingdom and his righteousness, and all these things will be given to you as well." Your heavenly Father wants to fill your life with His amazing blessings—real happiness and fulfillment, very likely including a wonderful marriage. But "all these things" come *after* you seek Jesus first. And the seeking doesn't stop once you become a Christ follower. Even after you've been guaranteed a place with Him forever, the seeking continues. Jesus wants to be first in every corner of your life, every moment of every day.

He wants to be first in your relationships. He wants you to pursue and relate to people according to His standards, not the lower standards of many around you.

He wants to be first in your finances, guiding your giving, saving, and spending according to His priorities.

He wants to be first in your day, receiving the best part of your time. Don't just fit Him in whenever it works out (if you even remember).

He wants His kingdom to be first in your heart. Before your car, your apartment, your clothes, and what you watch on television.

God wants your all. He rightly asks for a 100 percent commitment. His offer is an all-or-nothing proposition. And one of the benefits of your full devotion is that, when He's in His rightful first place, you experience fuller and fuller doses of His sacrificial love.

How did God show His love for you? He didn't send an angel to bring salvation. He didn't ask a superhero to rise to the occasion. He didn't send Jack Bauer to the rescue. He came Himself. And He didn't meet us halfway. He gave it all. One hundred percent. And He lovingly demands the same in return. "You must worship no other gods, but only the LORD, for he is a God who is *passionate about his relationship with you*" (Exodus 34:14, NLT).

And this loving demand from God shows up in marriages that go all the way. One important way we show wholehearted love to God is to lay down our lives (see John 15:13) for our spouses...day after day. Part of selling out to God is selling out to our spouses. It's worrying less about what they give us and much more about what we can give them—our all. That's the road to marriage intimacy and fulfillment. It starts with putting God unalterably first, and it ends with two people giving each other 100 percent.

LIFE BY THE NUMBERS

If Jesus must be *the One*, then what do you call your soul mate, your life partner, the man or woman of your dreams? You might think this is weird... That person would be...*the Two.*

That's right. The Two.

For every Christian, the One must be Jesus. Anything that pushes Him out of first place will threaten your success and fulfillment in life.

But once Jesus is in the right place, you're ready to put your spouse in his or her appropriate place. Second. No higher, no lower.

Your commitment to the One and your commitment to your Two are intricately bound together. You can't tuck them into their own neat, separate mental compartments or closets. That never works.

Loving the One is critically important to finding happiness with your Two. And loving your Two is one of the best ways to love the One.

MEETING *THE ONE*

The greatest day of my life was the day I met *the One*—Jesus. But my BC days weren't so good. I was a sophomore in college, on top of the world. For the first time in my life, I was popular. I played tennis for a small college with a student ratio of eight girls to every one guy. *God is good,* I thought. And so were my odds.

I'd joined a fraternity, was having a winning tennis season, and was making good grades. The partying couldn't have been better. And the girls couldn't have been wilder.

Everything was perfect—all I had ever dreamed of. Yet I was miserably empty.

I won't lie to you. The sinning was fun...for a while. Then it started to hurt, and hurt badly. That's what sin does. It compounds. It thrills, then kills. It fascinates, then assassinates. (Sin is like a good sneeze. It feels good coming out. Then you get snot everywhere.) Before long, my relationships started to break down, I developed a bad reputation, and hurting people became second nature.

Not so coincidentally, my fraternity got busted for beer and drugs and was put on probation. As part of our punishment, we had to host a Bible study. After drawing the shortest straw, yours truly was put in charge.

To say that people joked about *me* leading a Bible study would be the understatement of the millennium. With only a free pocket-sized Gideon New Testament, we started by reading Matthew 1. You want to talk about boring? Have you ever *read* Matthew 1? It's all about who begat whom. Nice start. (Imagine saying "begat" nowadays. "We got married and started begetting." See—it just doesn't work.)

The second chapter of Matthew was more interesting, but not nearly as interesting as our prayers. We were a bunch of wild frat boys who prayed wild-frat-boy prayers. We sincerely asked God to protect us while we partied and to keep our girlfriends from getting pregnant. (Try that prayer at the Baptist Student Union.) Most Christians would've laughed at the absurdity of our situation, but God was up to something.

Like many of my wild friends, I felt strangely drawn to Jesus. Was He who He claimed to be? Did He really love me? Could He really save me?

Hurting and lost, one night I cried out to Him. I prayed like I had never prayed before—deeply and passionately, with every part of my heart. It wasn't a prayer you'll ever see on a neatly printed Christian brochure or hear a television preacher pray. It was rough and raw. It was from the heart.

God, I hate myself and everything I stand for! I can't go on this way—hurting others and myself. If You're really there, I need to know. Show me. I can't take it any longer. Jesus, if You can really save someone, save me!

I didn't know what was going on, but Jesus was becoming my One—my Savior and my Friend. And suddenly everything was different. Forever.

If you've met the One, you understand what I'm talking about. You know the joy and peace of forgiveness...the thrill of following Jesus.

If you don't know the One—if you've never given your whole life to Jesus, the One who gave it all for you—do it now. Stop what you're doing and pray. In your own words, invite Jesus into your life. Tell Him you need Him and desire to please Him. Ask Him to forgive your sins. All of them. Cry if you feel like it. Let your tears of repentance and regret turn into tears of joy and acceptance. Commit your whole life to Him. Tell Him—and mean it—that He is *your* One forever.

I'd never tell you to seek the One because you desire a marriage that goes all the way. You seek Jesus because of who He is, not to get something from Him. But I'll remind you that you're far more likely to have the marriage God intends when He's the One directing you. Remember, the more you become like Him, the better prepared you'll be to give and receive His love.

Have you met *the One*? I hope so.

3

FINDING YOUR TWO

Does God's plan include only one *particular* perfect mate for everyone? You know, like in *Napoleon Dynamite,* when Kip found his one true love?

Kip, Napoleon's scrawnier, geekier brother, never abandoned the dream of finding his soooooouuul mate. Finally all his "chatting with babes online" paid off. Praise God for LaFawnduh!

But back to the question:

Does God have one special person for you? Or could God have *several* people in mind—any of whom could be great for you?

In my heart, I want to believe the romantic answer: "Before I was born, God created Amy just for me. We met. We married.

Now we're living our happily ever after." It sounds great. But I don't believe that's how God works.

Look at it this way. Do you think God puts the pressure of tracking down that one specific, "right" individual *on you*? And if you miss the right one, too bad—you can only choose a wrong one now. What if you marry the wrong person? You'd blow the whole system. With one "wrong" marriage, hundreds, thousands, millions...even billions of lives could be thrown into a tailspin.

Let's say God has planned for you to bump into your special someone tomorrow, while shopping for Double Stuf Oreo cookies. This is your chance. God's been planning this divine meeting since long before you were born. Everything is perfectly in place. Your future spouse is scheduled by God to be at the same store, at the same time, shopping on the same aisle.

You wake feeling especially close to God. You dress in your best grocery-shopping outfit and head for the local mega food store. Walking past the cereal toward the cookies, you see someone. *Wow! Could this be...?*

You come closer. Your eyes meet. You're about to speak. Your voice freezes. You panic. You choke. The moment passes. And so does the other person.

Nooooo! (This is the frustrated, fist-shaking, movie-hero-who-lets-the-bad-guy-get-away kind of "no.")

Disappointed that you didn't have the guts to speak, you grab your Double Stuf Oreo cookies and sulk to the checkout lanes. And in heaven God frowns and thinks, *Good grief. I had everything set up...and you blew it! Now you're destined to get fat eating Oreos all alone.*

The Secret Formula

I lived in fear of a similar scenario. Would I make a mistake and miss an opportunity that could guarantee my future marriage? *What if I missed God's moment?*

Once, when I was single, I saw an attractive girl at a mall, ice-skating gracefully to Christian music. For some reason I began to wonder if she was going to be my future wife. Finally, scared I'd miss my chance, I flagged her down. When she had glided over to the side of the rink, I asked her if she'd go to church with me. Instead, she invited me to do something to myself that I can't print in this book.

Yeah, she wasn't the one.

Fears like this are reinforced by the good-intentioned yet bad advice that floats around in the Christian community. And this advice, this "one and done" mentality about your Two, can actually keep you from having a marriage that goes all the way.

Many devoted Christ followers sincerely believe that no matter what they do or don't do, God will bring them mates. It's the "Magneto-Mate." Somehow "we'll just be drawn together." (That's like some misled believers who say, "I don't have to work. God will provide for me.") These ill-informed believers don't make any effort. Many don't go to places where other believers might be, and they don't try to improve their relational skills.

Some don't even take care of their appearance. They just sit around waiting...hoping...trusting God for a mate but never taking a single step in that direction.

Others are on the opposite end of the spectrum. Instead of waiting passively, they adopt a formula mentality: *If I do* a + b, *God will deliver* c. Many believe, *If I do everything juuuust right, God is obligated to bring me a mate.* Sincerely desiring to spend their lives with another, these believers religiously engage in daily devotions, rarely miss church, faithfully tithe, and remain sexually pure, hoping to get some leverage on God from their good works. If they dot every spiritual *i* and cross every relational *t*, then surely God has to produce Mr. or Miss Right. (Sure, these disciplines are important, but we can't reduce God to a cosmic Coke machine—push the right button and you get what you want.)

Personally, I've come to a couple of conclusions:

1. There may be several potential spouses with whom you could truly go all the way to God's best.
2. God wants you to do your part. Ever hear of free will? It's your life, after all—a loving gift from Him.

While these conclusions may crush some romantic dreams, they should also remove some of the pressure—even if you miss an opportunity for a relationship, God can provide another. One teacher said, "God presents qualified candidates, and you choose."

The Bible is full of examples of different ways couples met and married. Parents chose for their kids. God used a servant who went searching. Even after mistakes, God gave people second chances at relationships. These examples encourage me. When it comes to meeting your mate, there is no set formula.

But here's what we *can* say with certainty. God deeply values marriage. He loves you more than you can comprehend. And He's big enough to direct you toward a holy and awesome marriage. Philosophizing about decision making and the will of God can only go so far. At some point you simply have to move forward and trust Him.

So how do you choose a future life partner? What's the best way to search? And when you think you may have found him or her, how can you be sure?

To Date or Not to Date

Many capable authors have written books with different twists on dating. Joshua Harris wrote a book called *I Kissed Dating Goodbye.* His bestseller was followed by Jeramy Clark's *I Gave Dating a Chance.* The tension between different philosophies raises questions like: Should I date or not? Is courting better? (And what exactly *is* "courting"? If you don't know and you're a girl, read *Pride and Prejudice.* If you're a guy, skip the movie and watch Ultimate Fighting.)

I was fifteen and a half with my driver's permit when I was allowed to date a sixteen-year-old girl. Which, in my case, quickly led to trouble—my first "parking" ticket. I can still hear the cop's knuckles rapping on the car window. Pretty humiliating.

Dating has changed a lot over the years. The kids who are dating seem to get younger and younger, and they seem to be going farther and farther together physically. We've come a long way since the days when a young man would get on his horse and come calling on a young lady and then sit conversing with her and her family in the drawing room. Hey, we've even come a long way from my fifteen-year-old "parking" incident. Things sure have changed. But most of these changes aren't making our lives better.

You might think I'm going to build a case against "car dating"...or *any* dating. I'm not. Instead, I'm going to offer thoughts to help you find your spouse in a careful, God-honoring way, whether you date or not.

Guaranteed Grief

First, before you even *think* about any kind of close relationship, let's define one type of person you don't want to pursue—ever. If you're a follower of Christ, under no circumstances should you date a nonbeliever. To do so is to risk setting yourself and the other person up for unnecessary disappointment, maybe worse.

In case you're already arguing with me in your mind, let me take it even further. If the object of your affection isn't a believer, it doesn't matter if he's super cute or if she can sing, if he makes big bucks or if you both like U2, if she was a *Sports Illustrated* swimsuit model or if he makes Brad Pitt look ugly. Don't date a nonbeliever!

The most important criterion for a marriage candidate is a commitment to Christ. Jesus said in Luke 11:17, "A house divided against itself will fall." When I hear the word *division*, I think "two visions." Whenever a Christ follower marries someone who doesn't have a commitment to Christ, the believer is trying to build an already-divided house. Certainly this isn't the only way divergent visions can compromise a marriage union, but it's one of the most important.

If you set two builders to work on a house from opposite sides with two different sets of blueprints, the house wouldn't stand. The builders need to put their heads together, uniting their vision for the house. To go all the way, you must be united in partnership *under Christ*.

Some single Christians argue with me: "Do I really have to marry a Christian? I mean, I know this person who's so cute... and nice. And saying I can only date Christians just makes it so much harder to find someone."

My reply is always the same. "No, you don't have to marry a Christian. Unless you want to be happy, fulfilled, and blessed by God. If that doesn't matter to you, marry anyone you want."

I can't tell you how many times I've spoken to believers who break down, deeply expressing their heartache over being married to nonbelievers. Just this week I talked with a married mother of two. She explained how kind and moral her husband is. She's grateful for his faithfulness, stability, and provision for their family. But she's spiritually isolated and alone, unable to share her greatest treasure with her husband—her relationship with Jesus.

This is a mild example of maritally mismatched misery. The more extreme examples often include unfaithfulness, betrayal, fighting, discord, abuse, deceit, and divorce. Some believer-nonbeliever marriages may seem to work, but I'd never recommend one. The odds are simply stacked against you.

Narrow minded? Yes, very much so. In the same way, Jesus asks us to travel the narrow road (see Matthew 7:13–14), God's standard for relationships dramatically limits the field. Where does the narrow road lead? To life. How about the broad road, on which most travel? To destruction. The same is true with marriage. God has a narrow plan that works. But few people follow it.

Remember, we're doing something different. We refuse to be normal. We crave something distinctive—a marriage that goes all the way. So as Christ followers, we simply choose not to date or marry nonbelievers. It's not because non-Christians can't be admirable or moral people, but because ultimately they'll have different inner lives. Different values. A different vision for what life means at its core.

More to the point, look at what the apostle Paul once wrote to a group of believers who were having serious relationship problems. He said, "Do not be yoked together with unbelievers.... What does a believer have in common with an unbeliever?" (2 Corinthians 6:14–15).

If you're like me, you're probably wondering what on earth that means. A yoke is a farming device used a long time ago that rested across the shoulders and necks of two beasts of burden, joining them so they could work together, to plow a field, for example. That's no yoke. (Ugh!) Paul was actually referring to an Old Testament teaching: "Do not plow with an ox and a donkey yoked together" (Deuteronomy 22:10). A donkey and an ox are different sizes; the yoke would pull down painfully on the ox's neck and up on the donkey's. Also, they travel at different paces; one would continuously drag the other along. To yoke them together would be cruel to both.

The same is true when a believer and a nonbeliever are yoked—or joined—together. At first everything may seem fine. Over time, though, the fundamental differences in life values and vision will start to tear the relationship. It'll become impossible to keep in step with each other.

More than once I've refused to perform a wedding because one was not a Christ follower. Inevitably, both walk away angry with me. For example, years ago I decided not to officiate the marriage ceremony of a couple I'll call Keisha and Robert. Keisha had served God her whole life but wanted to marry a guy who hadn't. She told me how great he was…kind and considerate, with better morals than many Christians. He even agreed to attend church with her weekly. She was right. This guy was great.

But he didn't follow Christ.

When I refused to marry them (recommending they not marry at all), they got married at the courthouse. Keisha later explained how everything was great the first few months. But slowly they began to notice what appeared to be minor differences. Keisha wanted to tithe; Robert wouldn't dream of giving away 10 percent of what they made. After having their first and only child—a boy—Keisha wanted him in a Christian school. Robert insisted that public schools were just as good.

Although neither had committed any gross sins, their marriage was slowly tearing apart at the seams. They were simply two people with two different sets of beliefs.

Through tears, Keisha told me how moral Robert was. And good to their child. But the small differences became big. Constant fights about money. Repeated verbal jabs. Daily child-raising disagreements. Diverging visions about what really matters in life…

One day Robert told Keisha politely but firmly, "We're just not a good match. It's nothing personal, but we just have different goals." And he went his way. He's still involved in his son's life. He faithfully pays child support. He's civil to Keisha. But they're divorced. And Keisha is devastated.

Now Keisha's left asking, "Why didn't I follow God's Word?"

God's command is clear: don't be yoked together with unbelievers. Either we believe God or we don't.

Getting Friendly

Maybe you're dating a believer, but you know there's no possibility of marriage. Yes, the spiritual connection with Christ is the first and most important priority in choosing your spouse. But don't underestimate other valuable qualities. For example, chemistry is incredibly important and not at all unspiritual (more juicy info on this later). Sharing common interests always helps.

Even if the person is a committed believer, be honest with yourself. You might not be attracted. Or your personalities aren't clicking. (Like when you say something...then the other person hesitates a split second too long, throwing off the whole conversational rhythm. I hate that.) Perhaps you just have a distinct feeling in your gut—you like this person, but it'd be wrong to marry. Then don't string him along—for a movie, a meal, or to pass the time. Don't keep her around because she makes you look better or proves what a "man" you are. Honor every believer as a brother or sister in Christ. Don't use someone because he or she simply meets a need or feeds your ego. Love him or her enough to not mislead.

As a young guy, letting go of "this shouldn't be happening" relationships was a struggle for me. I'd occasionally allow friendships with girls to get too close. I knew deep down I shouldn't spend so much time with girls who were only friends. I suspected they liked me, and I allowed things to continue, inadvertently leading them on because I enjoyed their company. That was selfish and wrong.

Maybe you have a friendship with someone who falls into this category. You enjoy hanging out together, and you're "just friends." But you can tell the other person wants more. If you know you'll never marry this person, I'd strongly encourage you to limit how much time you hang out. As innocent as your friendship may seem, more often than not one or both people will become confused. It's certainly not wrong to have opposite-sex friends, but be wise.

Wait for Your LaFawnduh

So you've found the One. Now you're hoping for your Two. Exploring different friendships can be exhilarating, educational, and a total blast. Whatever you do, don't get in a rush. And don't sell out.

Suppose you go to the pound to adopt a dog. You see a nice mixed breed and decide to pet its head (somehow you fail to notice the foaming mouth). If the dog bites your hand and sends you to the emergency room with rabies, would you adopt it as your own personal Cujo? I doubt it.

If you wouldn't bring home the dog with the foaming mouth, why would you return to the wrong marriage material? or bring home a threat to your dream?

You're better than that. Jesus loves you. He's your One. And He will lead you to your Two. Don't settle for a third runner-up, fourteenth place, or the last-place straggler you have pity on.

Remember Kip? He could have easily done what many do: settled for a shortsighted and self-centered, "this one will do" kind of relationship. Don't do it. It may be tempting, but God has something better for you.

4

THE FRIENDSHIP FOUNDATION

After meeting the One during my sophomore year of college, I did something people thought was totally weird. And it was. But if I had it to do all over again, I'd choose weird every time.

Instead of dating women, I dated Jesus. (Hang with me. This will make sense in a minute. If not, the nice people in the white jackets can tell me what to do next.)

This was one of the most important seasons of my life. In the past, I'd struggled with sexual promiscuity. Because of this weakness and my new desire to please Christ, I stopped pursuing women altogether. Instead of chasing skirts, I chased after Christ and His presence. I made Saturday nights my "date nights." Most Saturdays I'd stay in my room reading the Bible, journaling, getting to know the One, preparing for my Two.

On my dates with Jesus, I sensed that He was truly preparing me for marriage. Purifying my mind. Cleansing me of selfishness. Teaching me to receive love. Making me someone who could give it.

Two years into this metamorphosis, I met a girl who seemed to have the hots for me. She was cute but not fully surrendered to Christ. When I refused to move forward with her, explaining that I wanted someone completely committed to the Lord, she called me a Bible thumper. My standards became her ammunition. (A Christ follower is always an easy target for ridicule.)

To my surprise, a few weeks later she told me about a girl who was, in her words, "just as overboard for God" as I was. Her name was Amy Fox. Even though that girl was mocking me, when I heard Amy's name, I believed she was the woman I would marry—and I told all my friends (*not* something I'd recommend—even now it seems a little crazy). This was before I'd seen a picture of her or met her in person.

Yeah, I know. Spooky. But what can I say? The last name "Fox" was like a sign from God.

For three months I prayed about whether to call this girl I'd never seen. Finally believing the time was right, I picked up the phone and dialed.

Would she be there? What would she think of a stranger calling? Could she really be...*the Two*?

Amy's answering machine picked up. *Gulp.*

Now, for what happened next, I need to remind you of the scene in *Top Gun* when Goose's wife says to him passionately after a few beers, "Hey Goose! You big stud! Take me to bed or lose me forever!"

Beep! I took the plunge. "Hey, you Christian babe," I blurted as confidently as I could. "Take me to church or lose me forever!"

Then I left my name and read a Bible verse.

The fact that Amy even agreed to meet me after hearing that message must be somewhere among God's top-ten miracles. (But for some reason I was so convinced she would be my bride that I recorded that first message—and then played it on our wedding day.)

The truth is, she was as much in love with God as I was. Jesus was (and is) her One. When we both became convinced that we had that in common, we knew we were moving in the right direction. Together we continue wholeheartedly to pursue Christ today. As a team.

So what happened between that crazy phone message and our wedding day? I'll share some of my story throughout the rest of this chapter as I describe what I believe is a healthy way to develop your relationship with someone who might be your Two.

Gearing Up for Your Two

What do you do next when you think you've met someone with marriage potential? Rent the movie *The Notebook* and celebrate? Obviously you'll want to spend time together.

Let me suggest a simple analogy that's been helpful to many. Think of the relationship as driving a stick shift with five gears. (Don't panic if you can't drive a stick!) You or the other person—or likely *both* of you—might feel an intense desire to go fast. You want to floor it! But if you want to succeed, you need to start in first, then move up gradually through the gears. This wisdom applies to you and every other driver, even NASCAR drivers.

A simple picture, I know, but when we're fogged by feelings and fantasies, simple is genius.

First Gear

When you're just exploring a relationship, beginning to get to know someone, you're in first gear. You'll want to start things very slowly, building a strong foundation. Consider the *m*-word *(marriage)* and the four-letter *l*-word *(love)* taboo. Why? They're just not the focus right now, and they're likely to do more harm than good. Your goal is simply to develop a friendship.

When you're interested in someone, it's normal to want to spend a lot of time alone together. But I'd advise against it. Whenever possible, participate in activities with groups of people. That allows you to see this person interact with others, and you'll learn even more about him when you see what his closest friends are like. Group time also takes some pressure off the early days of the relationship. Instead of ditching your friends and your previous social life, invite your new interest to participate in your world while you do the same in hers.

You'll also want to ensure that your relationship is pointed in the right direction—doing things together that would honor God. Psalm 25:4 makes a great prayer during this season of friendship: "Show me your ways, O LORD, teach me your paths."

For example, it's dangerous to center your relationship on the party scene. Start with the right foot forward, following God's paths—maybe a church activity, a day at the park, coffee at Starbucks, a scenic drive, or a nice lunch together. Avoid activities or places that invite premature speeding (prayer time in the backseat of a parked car, for example). These early days are hugely important because you're setting the tone for the rest of your relationship.

My friendship with Amy started on the phone. Then we decided to have our first face-to-face meeting. Our evening began at her church's youth group, where she was a leader. I got to meet her friends and watch her encourage kids. We didn't kiss. We didn't hold hands. We simply got to know a little about each other in a larger group. We each learned that the other had placed God first.

Compare that to the way Jim and Lacy met. Jim and his buddies had a few drinks before hitting the hottest bar in town. Lacy had on her most stunning low-cut top and a short skirt. Jim was seriously buzzed when he saw Lacy. He bought her a drink, then asked her to dance. After several more drinks and some grinding on the dance floor like two ferrets in heat, they left together and went to her place. You can fill in the blanks from there.

Which relationship do you think started with the best chances of long-term success?

Or consider the common scenario of Maya and Garrett. They were both so happy to have something new going with someone interesting that they felt like they were walking around in their own private world. And they were. As they spent every free moment together or on the phone, sharing every personal detail, they suddenly went AWOL from their previous lives. Old friendships dropped away. Old commitments too. Their relationship became their entire world as they moved quickly from long conversations to practically living together. A moment apart seemed too long. But not far down the road, Garrett realized he was reality-, space-, and oxygen-deprived. He sensed that what he and Maya had launched was not sustainable, or even desirable. And he wanted out.

In first gear, you start slow, limiting your interaction. You don't want your level of intimacy to race ahead of your level of commitment. You're not talking or texting daily. You're not holding hands or writing notes. Your new interest doesn't instantly become your top friend on MySpace. You're not talking intimately about your past. You're not playing "naked *Cirque du Soleil.*" You're developing a friendship, directed by wise guidelines, all the while guarding your heart and the heart of the one you're with.

This was one of the most important seasons in my relationship with Amy. I'll always treasure our early conversations, developing our friendship, without a bunch of expectations and pressure stacked prematurely on top of our budding relationship.

Second Gear

If you can sense God blessing your new friendship, you may consider shifting gears. In second gear, it's appropriate to spend a little more time alone together. This doesn't mean you abandon life as it was, leaving your friends and interests in the dust. Try to strike a healthy balance.

Continue to guard your heart. Here's where you could get way too excited, dreaming, hoping this could be your Two. Never forget to keep God first and acknowledge Him in all your ways (see Proverbs 3:5–6). Your imagination, emotions, and body can respond in nanoseconds. But it nearly always takes time to discern God's guidance on matters of this magnitude, so be patient. Don't put everything on the line.

Again, I'd recommend against romantic physical contact. (*Ohhhh man! I thought second gear was "up the shirt."* No, that's second base—and no, you don't want to go there.) I might sound boring and unrealistic. But think of it as being focused, considerate of the other person, wise, and uncommonly committed to the good future you really, really want. Physical touch exposes the heart and clouds the mind. So take things slowly.

You're still not talking marriage. The possibility may be at the back of your mind, but you're building the relationship. Discussing marriage prematurely puts too much pressure on you both. Instead of rushing toward the altar or letting your feelings dictate, you're moving into a stage of intentional discovery. It's time to ask questions like these:

- Is this person becoming more like Christ?
- Does this person have strong and growing character?
- Does this person have the right kind of friends?
- Is this person responsible—financially, relationally, emotionally, intellectually?

If the answer to any of the questions is no, perhaps you should put on the brakes and continue to focus on your relationship with God. Don't expect to lure him or her onto your path. By no means should you deviate from the road you're walking with Christ. If this person is not traveling with you, it's best to direct this relationship toward friendship, not something more serious.

But if you answer yes to all those important questions, go ahead and explore a little deeper:

- Is our attraction increasing? (It's not unspiritual to be drawn physically and emotionally to someone. I believe it's an important part of God's plan.)
- Are we helping each other grow closer to God, rather than drawing each other away from Him?
- Do people I respect think highly of this person?
- Do I believe God is blessing this relationship?
- Are we growing in our understanding of one another? Do we like what we see?

These are questions you need to discuss with each other, *after* a significant time together in second gear. If you both can answer all the questions with an emphatic yes, if your heart is warming toward this person, and if your optimism is mounting, then you might decide to shift into…

Third Gear

This is when you mutually agree to pursue the possibility of marriage. By now you know the character of the other person reasonably well. You're both seeking God, and you're enjoying each other. Now is the time to bring out the *m*-word.

Go ahead and openly discuss the possibility of marriage. As you do this, you should also intentionally…

- seek advice from mentors.
- read books about marriage.
- pray together.
- get to know each other's families.
- open up about your life, your hurts, and your dreams.
- talk about your possible future.

Now more than ever, you'll feel tempted to move forward physically. As your emotional attraction intensifies, so will your physical attraction. So where should you draw the line?

Though not everyone agrees it's possible, many committed Christ followers save kissing for marriage. Personally, I like the idea. (*Really, Craig? Where's the fun? This is gonna be a tough one for me!*) Kissing can be incredibly intimate. Once you get that close, you're almost certain to be tempted to do other things—especially when you start talking marriage.

In the first two gears, you guarded your heart—refraining from sharing verbally at too intimate a level. In third gear you rightly begin to expose your heart, but you must still guard your sexual integrity.

Amy and I struggled with sexual temptation, never going all the way, but certainly farther than we should have. As we opened up emotionally, we wanted to express our emotions physically. Trust me, your hormones will *hummm*! But I pray you'll keep the sexual parking brake locked for now. It won't be easy, but with God's help, you can do it.

If you haven't already, in third gear you'll likely discover some of the baggage the other person has picked up along the way. And they'll be noticing yours. *Pay attention to the baggage.* Too many people don't—especially when they're blinded by love (and probably a little lust too). Don't ignore the warning signals. If you see something you think could be a problem, chances are it will be. Not all problems are deal breakers, but at the very least, you both need to start preparing honestly for the challenging work to come. You might need to swallow hard and say, "I've enjoyed getting to know you, but this isn't working out."

Take Jeannette, a thirty-two-year-old HR director who'd never married. She was dating Adam—a thirty-eight-year-old divorced attorney and father of three. Though Adam was a committed Christian and very good to Jeannette, after four months of dating, she began to see warning signals. Adam had been divorced for two years, but every time he talked about his ex, strong emotions surfaced. Sometimes he'd cry. Other times he vented angrily. When Adam had his kids for the weekend, Jeannette often overheard him talking to them negatively about their mom. She worried a little about his emotional outbursts, but never having been married or divorced, she assumed it was normal behavior.

Their relationship progressed quickly. In the back of her mind, Jeannette began to fear more and more that Adam was still emotionally attached to his first wife, but she rationalized that their love would overcome the challenges. Five months later, they married.

All hell broke loose.

Adam and his ex continued their heated exchanges. Jeannette tried her best to be supportive, especially with her stepchildren, but everything she did was wrong. After eighteen months, Adam divorced her.

Jeannette is still recovering. She saw the warning signals, but she ignored them.

If you find baggage that concerns you, seek help. Get advice from your pastor, from wise mentors, or from a counselor. You might be able to work through the issues that stand between the two of you. Or you might be wiser to walk away.

Now, after all that gloom, it's important to acknowledge that in many relationships things progress much more smoothly. Once you both agree that God's directing you toward marriage, it's time for...

Fourth Gear

Engagement. What an exciting time! The proposal. The ring. The wedding date on the calendar. All the congratulations. The gifts. The wedding showers with vanilla ice cream in the punch. I love it, and so should you. But let me caution you: during the season of engagement, your top priority is not planning your wedding, but planning your marriage.

Work hard to remember that a reasonable wedding is over in an hour; a marriage is a lifelong commitment. Have a wonderful wedding. But put a hundred times more energy and time into planning for your marriage. Ask yourself, *Will the forty-seven hours we invest picking out the perfect centerpiece for our reception matter when we're navigating our first year of marriage?*

One couple I married, Jennifer and Torrence, asked all their friends with godly marriages to write letters of advice. While planning for their wedding, they studied about marriage. Reading dozens of these letters, full of years of wisdom, helped prepare this couple for a lifetime of love.

Remember, during engagement you're not married yet; rather, you're *planning* to get married. If you realize this isn't God's direction, it's not too late to respectfully shut things down. It's much less painful to break an engagement than to endure years in a bad marriage and maybe go through the soul-rending agony of divorce.

During engagement, I highly recommend premarital counseling or marriage preparation from your church. (I require all couples I marry to be mentored and take a class on marriage.)

Don't simply expect to figure out marriage principles along the way; aggressively seek them so you're leaps ahead from the get-go.

Here are a few important topics for your marriage-preparation discussions:

- career choices
- living arrangements after marriage
- financial plans—earning, budgeting, saving, and investing according to your shared values
- your developing philosophy for bearing and raising children
- your choice of the church in which you'll serve
- your plan to grow spiritually together

During engagement—*especially* during engagement—keep guarding your sexual integrity. (Did I mention that you're going to want to reach out and touch someone?) Many people work hard at purity up until this point, then let down their guard, thinking, *We're getting married anyway.* They're always sorry later. Keep Christ first, never neglecting your passion for Him. And protect the treasure of a wedding night with no regrets.

Fifth Gear

This is marriage. In the rest of this book, we'll study what a marriage in the will of God looks like, and how you and your Two can continue to grow in intimacy and fulfillment every year that you're together.

I like to say that Amy and I are living in overdrive, cruising together, pleasing God. Your marriage, built and blessed by God, will be one of your greatest joys on earth. Sure, you'll face challenges—sometimes huge ones—but with a strong foundation and the power of God's Spirit, your journey will be one of fulfillment, one you'll honestly thank God for.

Pop Goes the Question

Inevitably people ask, "How long should I date before marrying?" (I often look at eager couples and soberly pronounce, "You know, the Bible says not to marry until you've dated for at least five years." I try to keep a straight face for as long as I can.)

Truth is, there's no hard and fast rule. I always recommend that couples spend more time in gears one through three and have shorter engagements. Unfortunately, the opposite is often true. I frequently see two-, three-, and four-year engagements, and longer. This may work for some, but I believe it's wise to keep dating—the season of exploration—longer, and engagement—the season of serious preparation—shorter. Take all the time you need to make sure this person is God's Two for you. Once you're certain, proceed with engagement and marriage quickly.

Along the way, remember that if you travel too fast, you risk a painful, even life-threatening crash. Take things at God's pace. If at any time you know that the person you're with isn't God's best, do the right and wise thing, and gently end the relationship. If, on the other hand, you know that God is blessing your friendship toward marriage, then shift gears, following His pace and path, and enjoy the relational ride of your life.

5

SEXUAL MYTHOLOGY

Our misguided culture does have one thing right: sex feels good. Not just physically but emotionally. When you really care about the person you're dating, sex gives you a false sense of commitment. *He must love me to share himself so intimately with me.*

So if it feels good, why not just do it? Neither of you is objecting. You both have needs—physical and emotional. You care about each other. You feel the magnetism. And you're responsible adults.

Why say no to sex when yes is so easy?

It reminds me of my favorite boxers. These weren't Scooby-Doo boxers. They were shorts with a message—a gift at my tame but fun bachelor party. Printed all over my honeymoon underwear were the words *No, No, No, No, No, No.* But when you turned off the lights, beaming, glow-in-the-dark lettering appeared: *Yes, Yes, Yes, Yes, Yes, Yes, Yes!* My friends and I laughed until it hurt (but not as much as Amy did when I sported them on our honeymoon).

The light switch in our society is turned off, and the media proclaims its message to this generation in flashing neon: HAVE SEX. Have it often, with as many people as you desire. Have it with boys or girls—your choice. Hopefully you won't get pregnant—or get anyone pregnant—but if you do there are these clinics that'll take care of that little problem.

When it comes to sex, our society knows just one word: Yesyesyesyesyes! Unfiltered, uncensored, uninhibited *affirmative*!

To add to the problem, most of the time the advice coming from the Christian community is muddled, watered down, and out of touch. It's like the daytime message on my boxers: *No! No! No! No! Don't you kids be messin' around. No necking or heavy breathing. No truth or dare. No spin the bottle. No coed swim parties. No. No. No. No.*

Then when the church marries a couple, the message instantly changes. With the flip of a switch, it's suddenly *YES!*

And the well-intentioned young couple does their best to unlearn all of the church's negative, uninformed impressions about sex in one night.

Good luck.

Deliberate Delay

To be fair, the church has been so emphatic in its *"No!"* because of what God's Word says: "It is God's will that you should be sanctified: that you should avoid sexual immorality; that each of you should learn to control his own body in a way that is holy and honorable, not in passionate lust like the heathen, who do not know God.... For God did not call us to be impure, but to live a holy life" (1 Thessalonians 4:3–5, 7).

Amid the clamor of mixed cultural messages, God's truth blares like a siren. God wants us to avoid all sexual immorality, to learn to control our bodies, to not allow our desires to control us. God didn't call us to be impure, but to be holy.

However, honoring His principles doesn't mean you have to spend your entire life thinking sex is bad. Actually, there's a whole book in the Bible devoted to how good sex can be. The Song of Songs celebrates the sexual relationship of two people with some pretty graphic (and sometimes kind of funny) language.

> How beautiful you are, my darling!
> Oh, how beautiful!
> Your eyes behind your veil are doves.
> Your hair is like a flock of goats
> descending from Mount Gilead.

> Your teeth are like a flock of sheep just shorn,
> coming up from the washing.
> Your two breasts are like two fawns,
> like twin fawns of a gazelle
> that browse among the lilies. (Song of Songs 4:1–2, 5)

Hmm. Hair like a flock of goats? Last time I tried that one on Amy…it didn't work. And breasts like two fawns? That's just…strange. But to Solomon and his beloved, those were some sexy words. And along with all the Bible's teachings, all its "no's," God gave us those words to show us how blessed sex can be when it stays within His will.

This isn't about good or bad, it's about *order*. Sex obviously isn't bad, but it's only truly good when you follow God's path. I've said from the beginning of this book that any time we get things out of order, we're taking significant risks—and that's especially true when it comes to sex before marriage. I'm not talking about the obvious risks—sexually transmitted diseases, unwanted pregnancy, and the trail of hurt people left behind. Those dangers are obviously there, but they're not the *ultimate* reason you should wait for marriage to have sex. You should wait because it is God's will, His plan—and His plan is best. Not following it brings a much greater risk:

The loss of God's blessing.

And one future pain that few people consider is a marriage that fails to go all the way. All the way in intimacy. All the way in trust. All the way "until death do us part." All the way to the marriage God designed you to desire and experience.

The Great Sex War

I'll just go ahead and say it: there is *a lot* of sex in the Bible. Lust. Adultery. Homosexuality. Prostitution. Rape. And there's a good reason it's there. Throughout history Satan's forces have been on the attack. God's people often dodge the tempting ambushes. But other times, they're weak, vulnerable, gullible, or just plain rebelliously lustful.

The Evil One is always working to undermine God's plan. He wants us to believe that God's order doesn't matter. And lately it seems he's been more successful than ever. Two myths have become so prevalent in our society that even a lot of Christians are accepting them as truth. I think it's about time these myths got debunked.

Myth #1: You can have sex without consequences.

Birth control has been around for forty years now—long enough for it to become a normal part of everyday life. It's easy to believe that this science can shield us from the consequences of sex. And abortion clinics and morning-after pills offer ways to erase the consequences even after they've appeared—modern miracles to some. Heartbreaking to God. Even though it may be possible to rid yourself of some of the physical results of sex, you can't get rid of the emotional and spiritual results. You may be able to keep that baby from being conceived (or be able to get rid of it if it is), but the unseen outcomes are the ones no one ever talks about—and they're the ones that could hurt you most. Sex without *visible* consequences may exist. But sex without consequences doesn't.

Myth #2: You can have sex without intimacy.

What was once pursued in secret is now readily available from the nearest television and *Maxim* or *Cosmo* magazines, and literally anything you could imagine (or never want to imagine) is one click away on the Internet. The dehumanization of the people portrayed in pornography has made sex and intimacy two separate entities. Who needs intimacy, commitment, and marriage when sexual stimulation is readily accessible?

Wanting something real and genuine, we often choose a dangerous shortcut that appears more fun—a way for the sweet tooth to get straight from the appetizer to dessert and just skip all the healthy stuff in between. Following the pattern of sex without intimacy, many people today shun commitment and simply "hook up." It's becoming the norm to have friends with sexual benefits. Oral sex is the new french kissing. It's only after we've acted on the lie that we realize we've been ripped off and left with a bunch of painful consequences—not to mention the surprise guilt and shame. We wonder, *How did we end up here?*

Satan has taken a lot of ground. It's time to take it back.

WHY NOT?

Why should I wait? Why is God's way better? Why does the normal road lead to quick bliss and lasting bust? Why doesn't "going all the way" really go all the way?

With all the pressures and tensions we deal with—from inside and outside our bodies and minds, and from both the world and the church—is it any wonder we're confused? Is it any wonder that we ask…

Why? Why should we do things differently from most everybody else? Why should we do things God's way?

To Practice Faithfulness

When you're married, I'm sure you want to be faithful to your Two. But to succeed in that faithfulness, you must first learn to be faithful to the One. Hopefully, you've made (or will make) a commitment to holiness—a commitment that includes saving sex for marriage, controlling your body in a way that is holy, and staying away from all other kinds of sin.

It'll never be easy, but you'll gain more from your efforts than you realize. If you can keep your promise to God, you'll be so much more likely to be able to keep your promise to your spouse someday. And if you let the Lord down (because none of us is perfect), you can start over with Him. He forgives all if you ask—and then you can start practicing fidelity *again*, working even harder than before. Once you've had years of practice being faithful to the One, you will find that being loyal to your Two is almost second nature.

To Honor Your Future Spouse

Hebrews 13:4 says, "Marriage should be honored by all, and the marriage bed kept pure." Read that verse again. Who should honor the marriage bed? *All. All* includes you. *All* includes single adults. *All* includes married couples.

One way you can honor your spouse-to-be is by saving yourself for him or her—not just physically but emotionally. Be careful how you dispense both your heart and your body before marriage. Even while you're dating the person you believe will become your life partner, keep honoring that person by guarding his or her purity until you've publicly promised your lives to each other—on your wedding day.

To Gain Security

Even though Amy and I faced sexual temptation while dating, with God's help we controlled our bodies. It's difficult to describe the secure feeling that gives us. If we'd compromised sexually before marriage, I would probably worry that we might compromise after marriage. To this day, I've never worried that Amy might be unfaithful to me. She says the same about me. This restful confidence is one of the many reasons I'm thankful we waited.

To Spice Up Your Married Love Life

Most who fool around before marriage enjoy the short-lived rush of dangerous sex. Later, when they settle into marriage and a more normal sex life—an experience that would otherwise be immensely satisfying—they often feel let down. Where's the rush? the thrills? the danger?

But for the couple who waits until marriage, sex isn't only about the thrill. It's holy, special, intimate. Sex in marriage is about so much more than a pair of orgasms. It's about shared souls.

To Tell Your Love Story with Pride

My favorite blessing is *our love story*. For the rest of our lives, we (and many around us) will know that we honored God. With six children, I love that our message is "Do what we say, because that's what we did." We love to tell our story.

Too Close for Comfort

A wealthy widow who was becoming too old to drive safely put out an ad for a driver to help her get around town. Three applicants responded. She took the potential drivers to the back of her house and showed them her biggest challenge.

"If you'll notice," the lady said, "my driveway takes a very sharp turn around this brick retaining wall. Will you take a careful look at it?"

Each wannabe chauffeur touched the wall, acknowledging the obvious challenge for an aging driver.

"Just how good of a driver are you?" the woman asked each one. "How close do you think you can get to the wall without scratching or denting my car?"

The first man explained politely, "Ma'am, I haven't had a ticket or an accident in years. I can assure you that I can get your car within eighteen inches of the wall and never hurt your car."

The second guy stepped forward, proud and eager. "Ma'am, I'm sure he can do that, but I can do much better." Convincingly he continued, "Because I used to live in New York City, I specialize in driving in tight places. I can get within a foot of the wall without damaging your car."

The third guy shook his head. "I'm obviously not as talented as these gentlemen. If I were driving your car, I'd be so careful that I'd try to stay six or seven feet away from the wall, even if it took me several minutes to get out of the garage."

He got the job.

Some wonder how far we can go without actually sinning. A better approach is to wonder how far we can stay from temptation. Instead of asking, "How close can I get to the edge?" why not ask, "How close can I stay to God?"

Because you want to honor God…

Because you want to honor your future spouse…

Because you want to prepare for a fantastic marriage—a marriage that will go all the way…

Don't flirt with danger.

YOUR EMERGENCY TOOL KIT

Remember Bill Clinton's infamous "I did not have sexual relations with that woman"?

Evidence indicated that Clinton and Monica Lewinsky had engaged in oral sex. Apparently former president Clinton doesn't think oral sex is sex. Most young adults today agree. So how far *is* too far? Can we do "everything but"? Is oral moral?

Remember, if you want what few have, do what few do. Raise your standards. Pursue holiness. In Ephesians 5:3, the apostle Paul wrote, "Among you there must not be even a hint of sexual immorality."

What do you think a "hint" of sexual immorality would include? (I hope my bluntness won't offend you or make you blush. Sometimes speaking directly is best.)

For starters, a hint would cover more than just physical contact. It could begin with verbal flirting or sexually suggestive talk. A hint of sexual immorality would include watching inappropriate movies, together or alone. Certainly it would include rubbing someone sexually, even outside their clothing. Putting your hands under the clothing of someone you're not married to? Clearly two steps beyond the line. It shouldn't have to be said, but masturbating each other and oral sex outside of marriage are *way* past God's line of holiness.

With God's help, we'll pursue His standard: not even a hint of sexual immorality. But remember, even if you're strongly committed to sexual integrity, you'd be naive to believe that temptation won't affect you. Be prepared. When you're spending time with someone you might be tempted to go too far with, here are some so-practical-they're-pure-genius ways to keep out of trouble:

Keep four feet on the floor. This prevents leg wrapping, keeps certain body parts less accessible to others, and keeps your weight on the floor or seat, not on each other.

Keep your bed *your bed*. No sleepovers. No studying for finals on the futon. And as holy as it might seem, no praying together on the bed!

Keep everything buttoned and zipped. This standard is almost foolproof. No unlatching, unhooking, unbuttoning, undoing, untying, unzipping...no *un*-anything.

Keep your tongue in your own mouth. Admittedly, this is pretty extreme, even to a lot of pure-hearted Christians. I only offer it as a suggestion that's been helpful to many. Kissing is incredibly intimate. It should surprise no one that it often leads to other, even more intimate, acts. Amy and I didn't kiss for months. It wasn't until our first kiss that we were tempted sexually.

Remember those single people I mentioned who save their first kiss for their wedding day? Just imagine the passion that first kiss holds!

Recovering Respect

You may be thinking right about now, *Wow, Craig. Your advice is challenging, and I'm motivated...but it's already too late for me.*

To prepare sexually for marriage, you may have a lot of backtracking to do. I know I did. I had to unlearn a lot of false thinking, as well as proactively retrain my mind and heart.

But think about this: if you try in your own wisdom and strength to conform your mind back to purity, you'll fail. If I squeeze a Nerf football, I can change its shape however I want, until I get tired. As soon as I let go, it returns to football shape. The same is true for your mind. You can think pure thoughts with your injured mind for a while. But if all you bring to bear is your own effort, you'll likely slip back into distorted thinking.

You must protect your wounds long enough for *God* to heal your mind. You can't *conform* your mind back to God's standard of purity. Instead, God has to *transform* it. It's His work, by His power. With your willing submission to His healing presence.

Amy often talks openly with other women about healing the emotional wounds from previous relationships. Just as God can renew our minds, He can also heal deep, emotional wounds. For some, healing might come through prayer. For others, Christian counseling helps. For Amy, she spent time in God's Word, and His truth replaced the hurt and lies. No matter what you need, make sure you don't reopen a wound from the past with more mistakes. While you're seeking God for healing, guard the wound.

Here are a few practical pointers:

Guard your eyes. Like Job, promise to not look lustfully at another person (see Job 31:1). *What's the big deal if I look as long* *as I don't touch?* Jesus said that looking lustfully is committing adultery in your heart (see Matthew 5:27–28). Protect your wound by bouncing your eyes away from sexually stimulating sights.

This won't come naturally. It certainly didn't to me. But after years of hard work and training, my eyes now bounce away from the wrong places. After teaching this principle at church, I was in the gym when two girls from our church approached me. "Craig," they said, "we've been watching you this whole time, and it's true—you always bounce your eyes." It was kind of freaky to realize I was being so closely observed. Once I got over that, I realized the good news—my eye-bouncing training had come into play without my even thinking about it. You can train your eyes too.

Capture any sinful thoughts. The Bible instructs us to "take captive every thought to make it obedient to Christ" (2 Corinthians 10:5). Whenever your sin-damaged mind drifts to a wrong thought, stop, grab that thought, and make it obedient to Christ. Protect your wound from the further infection that comes with rotten thoughts.

You might have to walk away from your computer, turn off the television, cancel your fashion magazine subscriptions, or leave the gym. You may have to put down the romance books and stop fantasizing. Instead, pick up your Bible, call a friend, or go for a walk. Rather than dwelling on something impure, change your thinking (see Philippians 4:8).

Run from anything sexually tempting. And I mean *any-*

thing. We've already seen it: God says to flee sexual immorality (see 1 Corinthians 6:18). Don't try to fight it. Run from it.

In your premarried life, you can protect your wound by not fooling around, not falling into self-destructive masturbation, not viewing porn. With God's help, protect your wound, and He will renew your mind. Then when you do meet your Two, your mind will be free from focusing on the sinful past, free to dwell on God's purity.

If the best defense is a good offense, here are a few more tips for actively building your moral defenses:

Invite others to hold you accountable. Several guy friends spoke into my life regarding sexual purity. Accountability is essential to your purity. Find at least one close, trusted friend, and prayerfully tell all.

State your standards up front. A friend of mine tells any girl he dates his standards up front. "I don't fool around," he explains. Once he's given his word, he feels honor-bound not to back down from it.

Keep good company. Sure, as a Christ follower you'll want to befriend those who don't know Him, but if you spend time only with unbelievers, you'll get sucked down quickly. Make sure your closest friends are honoring Christ.

Repent quickly after failure. If you do fail, repent immediately. Turn to God, and receive His forgiveness and strength. Plan to avoid similar situations in the future. Tell someone you trust, and ask that person to pray for you.

Be warned. Your Enemy will attack you. Decide today how

you will defeat him. When you feel weak and stuck, remember, "God is faithful; he will not let you be tempted beyond what you can bear. But when you are tempted, he will also provide a way out so that you can stand up under it" (1 Corinthians 10:13).

Rest in God's protection, and fight in His strength. It's the responsible—and respectable—thing to do. Even if you've messed up in the past, you can make things right today, doing everything possible to prepare for your future marriage to go all the way.

6

THE PROBLEM WITH PLAYING HOUSE

Several years ago, I got a call from an old fraternity brother, Rick, who was now attending LifeChurch.tv. "Monica and I are going through some struggles at home," he said. "Would you be open to giving us some counsel?"

"Of course!" I replied, and we set a time to meet.

Three days later, Rick and Monica walked into my office, visibly tense. Almost immediately, Monica said, "He drives me crazy. Everything he does gets on my nerves. I can't take much more. I don't want to leave, but if something doesn't change soon, I don't know what I'll do."

Rick defended himself: "I'm not as bad as she says. It's tough living with Miss Perfect."

Monica prepared to fire back, but I interrupted. I needed to get some basic information first. "I'm so sorry you're struggling. With God's help, I know we can work something out," I offered. "First, tell me, how long have you been married?"

"Oh, we're not married," Rick answered. "We've lived together fourteen months." Neither of them felt the least bit uncomfortable telling me—their pastor—that they were cohabitants, not spouses.

"Have you guys ever considered marriage?" I asked gently.

They didn't "believe in marriage," Monica explained. She detailed their parents' divorces, including her dad's infidelity. "Getting married just doesn't seem necessary," she concluded.

Rick added, "We love church. And we're as committed as any married couple. After all, we're married in our hearts."

He continued, "We have an idea we think might help us. Would you conduct a special ceremony to bless our relationship?"

The "special ceremony" they requested wasn't a wedding. It was more like a house blessing or a baby dedication—something to make their relationship *feel* more official or garner more of God's favor for their lives. I guess I shouldn't have been surprised. As I've thought about it since, when you live together before marriage, you're saying by your actions, "I don't really believe in marriage." Not marriage by God's plan, anyway.

Inspiration struck. "Sure!" I answered. "I'd be happy to

write some vows to bless your living arrangement. Let's meet next week to talk them over."

They beamed.

The following week my old friend and his live-in arrived, glowing with anticipation. "Before I share your special vows," I said, "I wanted to talk a little more about the ceremony itself. I thought we'd have it at your home. Maybe invite some close friends and family."

Monica squeezed Rick's hand and smiled, obviously excited about the possibilities.

"Everyone will gather in your bedroom."

Startled, Rick and Monica looked at each other.

I plunged ahead.

"Here's how the vows will go," I said. "On your big day, I'll start, and you'll repeat after me. But for now I'll read the whole thing. Ready for your special relationship blessing vows?"

They hesitated for an instant, then both nodded. I read:

"I, Rick, take you, Monica, to be my cohabitant,

to have sex with you and to hold you responsible for half the bills,

to love and take advantage of you,

from this day forward, or as long as our arrangement works out.

I will be, more or less, faithful to you,

as long as my needs are met, and if nothing better comes along.

If I should break up with you, it doesn't mean this wasn't special to me.

Because I love you almost as much as I love myself,

I commit to live with you for a while.

So help me…me.

In the name of sex, options, and selfishness, amen."

I knew I had taken a huge gamble. I prayed silently.

I was met with blank stares.

After what felt like an eternity, Rick gently took Monica's hand. Softly, sincerely he said, "We need to go. We have some things to talk about." And they left.

The next day Rick and Monica walked in without an appointment. *They hate me*, I thought, and cringed, waiting for the worst.

"We always *thought* we were committed." Rick glanced at Monica, then turned to me. "Your vows sobered us up. We don't want what we thought we wanted. We want God to bless us."

Monica asked if I'd marry them. I couldn't have been more delighted.

Fuzzy Logic

Once a couple truly commits, before long one or both start to reason, *Why are we paying bills at two places? Moving in together would be so much cheaper.*

It makes sense, doesn't it? According to conservative studies, almost half of non-Christians live together before marrying. Not surprising, right? Without a biblical worldview, living together sounds viable. What's surprising is that one in four

Christians—you, me, and people we love and know—follow the same reasoning and move in together before walking the aisle.

Although I never shared an address with a girlfriend, before I surrendered to Christ I seriously considered living with my last one. We practically lived together anyway. I remember thinking, *Hey, I pay $450 a month plus bills, and she splits rent for $500. That's stupid! We're in love. We could test-drive marriage. If it works, we'll just take the next step. Besides, I've seen what divorce does. That's not happening to me. Some people may look down on us, but it's our business. We're committed in our hearts. That's what matters.*

It all seemed so innocent. So logical. So friendly.

Which reminds me of a friend my son made.

I recently walked onto my porch and saw my three-year-old, Bookie, jumping excitedly, singing and pointing. "My fwend! My fwend! I wuv my fwend!"

I'd never seen him that worked up. Curious, I walked over to see his "friend." My heart stopped. Bookie's new friend was a young rattlesnake. I snatched Bookie away before the snake could strike. Then I crushed the snake's head with my shoe. (After chopping the head off with a shovel.)

What appeared innocent—even friendly—was in fact deadly.

A wise man once said, "There is a way that seems right to a man, but in the end it leads to death" (Proverbs 14:12). We sometimes want so much for something to be right that we're willing to live in denial of the very thing that could kill the relationship.

We sometimes miss the clarity of God's logic because we're getting pressure from the other person. For example, one person might begin to play the "If you really loved me" game. You know that game. Dating couples play it just before wrecking their relationships.

"If you really loved me, you'd stay."

"If you really loved me, you'd move in."

If your boyfriend or girlfriend tries manipulating you into something wrong, warn them that they're risking losing you. You live to please God, and you won't compromise His standards. If they can't live with that, they'll have to live without you. A manipulative relationship is dangerous, especially when it can lead to losing those treasures that you value most.

And what are some of your most precious treasures? Your reputation. Your example. The trust of family and friends. Your purity. Your future marriage bed. The love story your children and grandchildren will ask you to tell one day. And above all, the unhindered blessing of God. Cohabitation before marriage puts some of your greatest treasures on the line.

Guard your treasures! Don't compromise, or you might destroy the relationship and your lifetime together. Moving in together may seem right. After all, you really want your relationship to last. But this path toward what you want most can actually lead to losing it.

Ominous Odds

If you think you're improving your odds of getting married by sharing a home with your boyfriend or girlfriend, you're wrong. Half the couples living together right now will break up within five years. And more than 60 percent will break up within ten years, according to a 2002 study by the Centers for Disease Control and Prevention. And only 40 percent of people who live together actually get married.

Living together may make you *feel* secure. But that kind of security is a phantom. Even for those who do marry after living together, the statistics are grim. The divorce rate for people who live together before marriage is at least 33 percent higher than for those who don't.

You might be one of those who say, "Well, Craig, the reason I'm living with my significant other is that I'm not sure about love or marriage. I think it's wiser not to commit. If we don't end up married, then it will be the right thing, and at least it won't hurt so much when we split."

With so many couples getting divorced these days, I don't blame you for being hesitant. But if you are asking God to guide you in your relationships, and you're making a conscious effort to follow His will, you should trust Him to get you where you need to be—and to help you recover if something does go wrong. The problem with living together is that, by your actions, you're telling God you think you know better than He does—that your truth is better than His. You're choosing to not trust Him with one of the biggest decisions of your life. And if you don't trust Him, you won't be able to receive His blessing.

Certainly some live-in partners do get married and enjoy long and meaningful lives together. That's the way the world works. A principle is not a guarantee or an equation. The book of Proverbs makes it clear that fools sometimes succeed, cheaters sometimes prosper. But exceptions to a rule do not invalidate that rule. As a rule, fools and cheaters—even really nice ones with warm, fuzzy intentions—lose. Life just goes better when we value wisdom and integrity. So if you're resisting biblical truth on this issue and nothing terrible has happened yet, I urge you to carefully reconsider.

Our life choices have consequences. God wants to bless you. But He won't bless sin. If you've become one of His by choosing to follow Christ, He won't reject you completely. When we pursue destructive lifestyles, our patient and merciful Father may let us follow our own ways for a season. But His patience doesn't negate the consequences that are piling up. Sooner or later, they will be ours to deal with (thankfully, with the help of a loving Father who never leaves us).

If you're living together, it's time to decide. I won't lie to you: your decision will be very difficult. But it'll be one of the biggest ones you ever make. Do you love this person? Do you really believe this is whom God wants you to marry? If not, call it quits *now*. You may hesitate, not wanting to hurt your lover. But you're *already* hurting that person, and yourself. Avoid any more pain and wasted time. You're doing the merciful, truly loving thing to break up today. (We'll talk more about how to do this later.) If, however, you believe this person is your Two, start treating him or her the way God desires. True love will do the hard thing, the right thing.

Now, it's commonly thought that the "right thing" for those living together is to marry immediately—to "make each other honest." Let's slow down and think this through. If you've been sexually involved, you've entered a mental and emotional fog. Sexual intercourse is more than biology at work—it's a merging of souls. That means it affects you more than just physically. It stirs your emotions. It clouds your judgment. It literally changes your brain chemistry.

If you're under the "spell" of sex, do you really think you can discern whether you're right for each other? Your sexual and emotional involvement has made you *feel* right together. That's very different from *being* right together.

Take a Hard Right

In any case, the hard, right thing—right now—is to stop having sex. Move out. I know it's expensive. It's inconvenient. It's challenging. It's embarrassing. But it's better than missing God's best, maybe for the rest of your life. So *move.*

How about a cooling-off period? Give each other some space. Seek God, and soak yourself in your true identity in Him. Allow Him to reclaim your mind and emotions. Let the fog dissipate and your feelings emerge from the influence of sex's high. Taking a few months to achieve clarity is a small price to pay to ensure that you embark on a life commitment, not a life sentence.

While you're trying to discern whether you have, in fact, met your life partner—make three promises. You might express them verbally or in writing or both:

I love you so much that I'll never ask you to compromise. *Because you're so special to me, I promise never to do anything to hurt your reputation. I'll never push you sexually. I'll never ask you to do anything outside God's will.*

I love you so much that I won't hurt your relationship with God. *I won't do anything to damage your intimacy with God; I'll help you grow closer to Him.*

I love you so much that, if God leads, I'll devote my life to loving you in marriage. *Up to this point, we've been saying "maybe" to each other. We've been doing married things while keeping our options open. If we marry, from that point on my "yes" to you will always be "yes." Outside of marriage, my "no" to sex will always be "no" (see Matthew 5:37). As God leads, my commitment will become, "Yes, I promise to love you as Christ loves the church" (see Ephesians 5:22–33).*

If you've made mistakes, and if you're in pain because of them, don't lose hope! God is the God of second chances (and third, fourth, and five hundredth). Yes, you've blown it. But God wants you back. And He can genuinely change your desires, your habits, your patterns of thinking and living. He's that powerful. He's that loving.

God will show you His grace. It's not too late to experience His best.

No Harm, No Foul?

Before we move on, I want to address a somewhat related topic. You might be thinking, *Hey, we're not living together. We occasionally stay the night, but we're not having sex. For us, it's just talking late into the night, snuggling. And what a blast waking up together (except for the morning breath)!*

And it's true. Staying the night with your girlfriend or boyfriend can be a lot of fun. So can road trips together, weekends away...or at home.

But just because it's fun doesn't mean it's smart.

How would I know about coed sleepovers? Well, before I was committed to Christ, having girls stay the night was as common as drinking cheap beer. In those circles, having your girlfriend stay over wasn't just common, it was expected.

Usually the first sleepover wasn't planned. I'd meet a girl at a party, hit it off, and stay out late. Not wanting the evening to end, we'd go to my place or hers. Before we knew it...morning. I'd just spent the night with a virtual stranger...again.

A lot of people do this. Often the sleepovers involve sex. Sometimes they don't. Someone might argue for a nonsexual sleepover: *It's no big deal. Are we hurting anyone? We just want to be close. We just want to talk. Snuggle maybe. No sex. Honest.*

We've already looked at Hebrews 13:4: "Marriage should

be honored by all, and the marriage bed kept pure." Obviously this rules out lovemaking outside of marriage—for both single and married people. But the intimacy of the marriage bed involves much more than the sex act, and protecting that intimacy rules out a lot of behaviors besides sex.

For example, would Amy mind if, while she was out of town, I had another woman stay the night? *Yes.* What if we promised not to go all the way, just fool around? You know, we can look in the barn but not go in. Again, yes. What if I promised we wouldn't do anything sexual? Just innocent companionship. Wouldn't that be okay? *No.* Why not? The marriage bed must stay pure. Sleeping in the same bed, prolonged physical contact, deeply personal conversations—all are intimate acts, reserved for marriage.

If it's right for me to carefully guard these nonsexual intimacies with my wife *in* marriage, why should it be any different for you *before* marriage? Your future marriage needs your protection now. You need to guard *all* aspects of that intimacy—sexual and nonsexual—if you want to experience the pleasures of purity and trust in your marriage bed.

And that's assuming you're actually able to stop before sex. What at first seems innocent can quickly slide into the territory you were sure you could avoid. The Bible actually says to avoid even "*all appearance* of evil" (1 Thessalonians 5:22, KJV). For Christians, even if sex is avoided, sleepovers mean compromised testimonies and possibly causing others to stumble.

THE RIPPLE EFFECT

Several months after my commitment to follow Christ, I promised God that my next sexual encounter would be my honeymoon. When I met Amy, I told her the same thing, and she enthusiastically agreed. We decided from the beginning: (1) zero sex and (2) zero sleepovers. Although we held to the first commitment, I'm sorry to say we compromised on the second.

And jeopardized our relationship.

As a financially challenged college student, I was motivated to approach our dates creatively. One day I told Amy we were going camping, but I'd have her home by midnight. I brought her to my home, where I'd turned my living room into a makeshift campsite, complete with tent, sleeping bags, picnic dinner, and stuffed "wild" animals. She loved it.

We ate dinner, made fireplace s'mores, read the Bible, prayed, and talked. Midnight snuck right past us. At 2 a.m. I knew I had to get her home, but we didn't want the night to end. So we kept talking. Until, without meaning to, we both fell asleep. The next morning's sun woke us. We blinked at each other, beginning to grasp the significance of what had happened.

Amy had just stayed the night.

That first compromise opened a dangerous door we hadn't intended to open. One sleepover led to another…and another. Eventually we crossed some physical boundaries, never "going all the way," but we definitely went too far. Our behavior was threatening to destroy the potential to truly go all the way. I knew we were not pleasing God. Deeply grieved and ashamed, I finally told Amy we should probably break up.

I'm eternally grateful to God and a few mentors, who helped us work through that self-imposed danger. But we hadn't prevented all the damage. Later, when I thought we finally had everything under control, I realized people were talking. They believed I'd reverted to the old Craig.

What's more, we later learned that another dating Christian couple, seeing our bad example, started spending nights together. They wound up pregnant. To this day, I wish we'd been better examples.

CLUCK OR OINK?

Are you ready for a real commitment—a commitment as strong as any you've ever made? Are you a chicken, or are you a pig?

A farmer once wanted to make breakfast for his family. He strolled to the barn, told the animals his plan, and asked for volunteers. Chicken quickly strutted up and offered, "Dear Farmer, you know I love your family. I'll help!" The other animals fell silent for several awkward minutes. Finally, Pig squealed quietly, "Great Farmer, you're always kind and generous to me. I'll also help."

Later that morning, Chicken proudly peered through the farmhouse kitchen window, watching the family eat breakfast.

But Pig was not beside her. The family was enjoying eggs and ham. Pig's words meant so much more than Chicken's.

Chicken was *involved.* Pig was *committed.*

Are you ready for a real commitment—a commitment as strong as any you've ever made? Being involved and being committed are miles apart. In our world today, most people are relationally involved, but few are truly committed. If you want a marriage that goes the distance in every way—the marriage that God fully desires for you—being involved isn't enough. You need to be committed.

I'll bet you never thought someone would tell you to be a pig.

7

HOW TO HIT THE "BREAKS"

You may remember the old Neil Sedaka song "Breaking Up Is Hard to Do." (Or maybe like Usher says, you just "gotta let it burn." Either way, I'm sure you'd agree with the sentiment in the song title.) It's become a catch phrase in our culture, partly because the title tells the truth. Personally, I wish Sedaka would have followed that song with another: "Staying with the Wrong Person Is Even Harder." I know it would've been a hit.

We dread breakups for good reasons. One is the painful experiences of past breakups, especially when you were the break*ee*, not the break*er*. The other person tried to let you down kindly, carefully, but you could see through all the evasion and indirectness straight to the truth, and it hurt. Maybe he said, "I just want to date other people." But you knew he really meant,

"I'm looking to see if I can find someone better." Or she said, "Let's just be friends." But how could you possibly consider a mere friendship with someone you cared about so much?

Or he said, "It's not you—it's me."

Sure.

Who wants to go through that again? Or put someone else through it? Many times we delay (or avoid) breaking up because we're hoping to spare the other person's feelings. Sometimes we just don't want to be alone.

I had a serious girlfriend in college. She was fun. She was cute. She was popular. But she wasn't God's best for me. Deep down I knew it, but I didn't want to admit she wasn't right for me. Maybe you can relate. Perhaps you're with someone you enjoy. He or she has a lot going on, but if you're honest, you can admit that your relationship isn't going anywhere. It's time to end it.

On the other hand, maybe you're with someone who has potential, and you're not sure if you have a future together. At times you want to cut and run. A day or two later you think, *Maybe—just maybe—this could work.* Occasionally you can't imagine anything better; you're ready to walk the aisle.

Polly and Seth are facing this very dilemma right now. They're a great couple who've been dating for a year and a half. They're fully committed to God's standards and have a good relationship, but they're not sure if it's God's plan for them to marry. They're wondering, if they do marry, will their marriage go all the way?

How can you know? Really know? The answer is different for different people.

If you're currently in a serious relationship, you should work toward two goals:

First, decide whether you should stay with your boyfriend, girlfriend, or fiancé(e) or whether you should break up. Second, if the answer to the breakup question is yes—if you're with someone who's less than God's best for you—I want to help you understand the healthiest, most God-honoring way to end the relationship. It won't be easy, but if the two of you aren't right for each other, it's time to hit the "breaks."

Danger Ahead

Let's start with two situations in which you should definitely break up. The first is when your girlfriend or boyfriend lives consistently without integrity. Integrity covers a lot more than just that he or she is nice and makes you feel special. A person with integrity measures his or her inner desires and values by the standard of God's truth—and that inner commitment is matched by outward behavior, even in the little things that no one else sees.

Integrity matters because, for one thing, it determines where you're going and how you'll get there. Proverbs 11:3 puts it bluntly: "The integrity of the upright guides them, but the unfaithful are destroyed by their duplicity."

Destroyed. That's a pretty serious consequence. When a person lacks integrity, it's only a matter of time before the systematic self-demolition begins. Anyone nearby gets sucked into the destruction. No one is immune. Not even you.

If my assessment sounds overly definitive, it's because I have *a lot* of firsthand experience—on both sides of the pain. For years, I was "Craig the Inflicter." Before I was a Christian, on the integrity scale I scored probably about a negative nine hundred. Lying felt normal to me. Stealing was second nature. Deceiving was like breathing air. Though I fooled myself into believing I was a good guy, I really wasn't. I was a bad guy who hurt and disappointed a lot of people.

For some sick reason, some girls seem to be attracted to "bad boys." A few of these girls were attracted to me. For the rest of my life I'll regret what I did to them. It would be inappropriate to describe my behavior in detail, but here's the short version: These girls were convinced I was a good guy who cared. In reality I was playing them. Often I was dating more than one girl at a time and leading others on. I hurt a lot of good-hearted young women. What I did was wrong, and I'm deeply sorry.

But what goes around comes around. I also dated my share of integrity-lite girls. Most of them drank heavily and slept around; some used drugs. All the makings of disaster. And I got burned many times.

I hope you haven't had personal experience with someone like that. Maybe you have. By now you might be smart enough to run from the obvious ethical offenders. But what about the not-so-obvious ones? Individuals who are generally moral, but suffer occasional lapses in integrity?

Well, I'm not perfect. Neither are you. Maybe we shouldn't expect someone else to deliver perfection when we can't do it ourselves. Remember, we're not searching for perfection but for someone who is saying to God in his or her life, "Lord, change me. Make me more like You." When your girlfriend or boyfriend does something against God's Word, see how quickly he or she repents. A good mark of maturity is a short time span between sin and repentance. If she lies, admits it quickly, and asks for forgiveness, she's on the right track. If, on the other hand, he lies, covers his tracks, lies again, then yells at you for not trusting him…you have a problem.

Watch the little things. If she'll cheat on a test, she might cheat on you. If he fudges on an expense report at work, he might stretch the truth with you. Even though a sin may seem small, it could be the seed that grows to choke out your future marriage. No matter how much you enjoy this person, no matter how good-looking he or she is, and no matter how badly you want to be married, if the person lacks integrity, call it off.

Do it compassionately. People in sin are certainly experiencing their own pain because of their behavior and are likely unaware that they're bringing it on themselves. But you have to protect yourself and your future marriage.

A second situation in which you should definitely terminate a relationship is when your boyfriend or girlfriend drags you into sin and away from God. The Bible says, "Bad company corrupts good character" (1 Corinthians 15:33). Bad company doesn't just take other bad people further down; it darkens the hearts and souls of decent people. If that doesn't jar you awake, listen to Proverbs 21:16: "A man who strays from the path of understanding comes to rest in the company of the dead." Are you beginning to see a pattern here? Destruction? Even death? This is serious business.

Before I was a Christ follower, I pulled my girlfriends into sin-saturated settings. We went to parties that didn't honor God, watched movies full of garbage, and did things that offended God. I even dated some very nice, moral, Christian girls. They never converted me, but several of *them* ended up doing things they hadn't planned on. If we started out with nothing in common, we usually ended up sharing one thing—sin. Why? Because I was bad company.

If you're with someone who pushes you into sin—dishonesty, drugs, alcohol, rebellion, sexual immorality, law breaking—don't fight it. *Run from it.* This is especially true with the hypnotic allure of sex. The Bible says to flee all sexual immorality (see 1 Corinthians 6:18). But any type of sin is dangerous. If the person you're dating lacks self-control in one area, he'll likely lack it in several other areas. If she demonstrates a track record of self-gratification, she's on the way down a deadly path. You don't have to go along. Break away!

Ask yourself, *Is dating this person drawing me closer to God?*

Or am I finding myself drawn away from Him? Don't flirt with anyone or anything that hurts your walk with Christ.

We've already talked about the almost guaranteed grief that results from a Christ follower marrying an unbeliever. This is a good place for a reminder. If your boyfriend or girlfriend isn't committed to Jesus, the two of you are trying to build a life together using different sets of blueprints—two opposing worldviews, two conflicting sets of values. Chances are great that this person will pull you away from God, not that you'll pull the person closer to God. If your life is surrendered to Christ, and his or hers isn't, I'm sorry to say this, but to continue the relationship is cruel for both of you.

Where There's Smoke...

Along the route from my office to my home, a street sign warns Slippery When Wet. I'm grateful for that sign. It tells me that when I see certain conditions, I should be watching for danger.

Do you see evidence that you're in a slippery relationship? Here are nine warning signs:

1. **Your friends and parents are opposed to the relationship.** When the people who love you think you're making a mistake, chances are pretty good they're right. Listen to wise counsel.
2. **Your boyfriend or girlfriend has bad relationships with his or her parents.** Yes, there are exceptions. But

unhealthy family relationships are often indicators of broader and deeper issues.

3. **He or she doesn't maintain any long-term friendships.** If your boyfriend or girlfriend can't keep friends, he or she probably won't keep you and may have difficulty with relationships in general.
4. **He or she is obviously drifting away or running from God.** You can't make conclusive judgments about what's in someone's heart, but you can get a pretty good idea by watching for spiritual fruit (see Galatians 5:22–23). Even if he labels himself a Christian, if you don't see evidence of God in his life, don't proceed.
5. **He or she is overly jealous.** Some possessiveness might be expected. But keep in mind that an overly jealous person usually doesn't trust himself and will likely cling to you, expecting you to provide the security that only God can provide. If she's always worried about your loyalty, she may not be willing to cultivate the trust that leads to genuine intimacy.
6. **He or she is not financially wise.** This may not seem like a big deal now, but one day your financial survival and well-being may be threatened by it. Disregard for wise stewardship will likely lead to a lifetime of marital struggles. Don't date someone who refuses to live on what he or she makes.

7. **He or she often tears you down.** You should feel better about yourself when you're together. If you don't, this probably isn't the person God has for you. You're too special to subject yourself to a lifetime of belittling.
8. **He or she is prideful.** Pride is an enemy of intimacy. If he looks down on others, doesn't receive criticism well, or always has to be right, prepare for a lot of misery or get out now.
9. **He or she kisses funny.** Just joking. Well, sort of. As you grow in your relationship, your attraction will likely grow too. If it doesn't, you might still have a good marriage, but in most cases my guess is that God has someone else for you.

Steps to Good-Bye

Right now you might be panicking, especially if some of these warning signs are telling you that you're in a harmful relationship or in a relationship that just isn't God's best. Maybe you've come to the uncomfortable realization that you're walking the wrong path with the wrong person.

Two of my close friends, Luke and Ginger, were seriously considering marriage. They even attended a marriage-prep class and shopped for rings. Luke confided in me and Ginger confided to my wife that they both desperately hoped this relationship was in God's plan. But deep down, each of them felt that something wasn't right. Luke worried about Ginger's frequent outbursts. Ginger worried about Luke's lack of life direction.

Even though they wanted to get married, they realized they couldn't *hope* their way to a marriage that goes all the way. Three years later, Luke and Ginger are both happily married—to different people. They're both so glad they paid attention to the warning signs.

If you're tempted to dismiss all the red flags, remember what's at stake. The fact is, you can't marry the best when you're dating the runner-up. While you're searching for Mr. Right, don't settle for Mr. Right Now. Or you might be too preoccupied to see Mr. Right when he walks by.

Maybe you're finally accepting the reality: you have to break up. But how? You've seen ugly endings. Lovers turned enemies. What's the best way to end a relationship and honor God in the process? Four thoughts:

1. **Talk face to face.** You owe your boyfriend or girlfriend that much dignity. Don't break up over the phone. Don't text a breakup message or send a Dear John e-mail or letter. (That's for wimps.) Do it in person. When the time comes, observe a couple of other simple rules: Try not to break up when you're angry, or you may say things you'll regret. After it's over, never talk badly about the other person.
2. **Tell the truth in love.** The Bible is clear: We don't lie. We tell the truth, lovingly. When I became a Christian, I broke up with a non-Christian girl and told her it was

because I would only date believers. Years later, she committed her life to Christ. I learned later that one of the main reasons she was drawn to Christ was the way I ended our relationship. I had treated her gently, but I told the truth.

3. **Draw the line without shaming yourself.** This may be tough. You don't want to hurt anyone. Breakups usually hurt terribly, especially for the recipient. But if this person isn't for you, the converse is just as true: you're not right for this person. To stay with someone would be unfair to the person whether he or she realizes it or not. Tell the person without taking a guilt trip.
4. **Stand firm.** When God leads you to break up, do it and let it stay done. When loneliness settles in, don't call or visit. That's unfair and selfish. Be firm. You should probably limit your contact for good. Once, I signed a commitment to God to not go back to an old relationship, and I carried my written vow in my wallet as a reminder.

Life Goes On...

You may realize it's time to end a wrong relationship. Or the one you're with may call it quits. What you do immediately following a breakup can make or break your future.

My wife counseled Shannon, a young woman who'd recently

ended a two-year dating relationship. Shannon asked, "What am I supposed to do now? I spent all my time with my boyfriend. How can I fill that void? How do I move on? And how can I keep from making another relationship mistake like this?"

Although I don't have any perfect formulas, I'll offer some suggestions.

You might feel like your world is crashing down. That's not unusual. Ending a relationship is often like experiencing a death. It's a significant loss. And the more and the longer you were joined physically and emotionally, the greater the loss. Grieving is normal and healthy. If you feel like crying, cry. Cry a lot if you need to. Then cry some more.

At the same time, I hope you'll sense God's encouragement and presence. The Bible says His Holy Spirit is the Comforter (see John 14:26, KJV). While some who experience a relational loss tend to go off the deep end into wild living, instead draw close to God. If you've drifted from Him, renew your relationship. Seek Him. He will show Himself to you.

I'd also encourage you to stay active. If you start to feel depressed, it's tempting to shut out the world and stay home alone. Get out and do something fun or productive outside yourself. Exercise. Go to church. Serve in the inner city or in your neighborhood. Volunteer at a crisis pregnancy center. Do something to make a difference in other people's lives, and you'll start to feel better about yourself.

With time, you'll begin to heal. I promise. And as you do, evaluate what you learned from the relationship. Don't just focus on what the other person did wrong, but examine what you could do better in the future. Ask yourself questions like these:

- Did I ignore any early warning signals? If so, what do I need to watch for in the future?
- Did I stray from God in this relationship? If so, how can I stay close to Him in future relationships?
- What will I do differently next time?
- What did I learn about myself?
- How did God use this experience to prepare me for a marriage that will go all the way?

FREE

If you're dating someone you know isn't right for you, put this book down and end the relationship. Go into the next room and talk to them. Or go meet them somewhere and have the talk. Do it now. If that's not possible, prayerfully prepare your heart and your words, and determine the time and place. Maybe call someone you trust to hold you accountable to follow through.

Lovingly let go of the counterfeit.

Free yourself to receive the real thing.

8

YOUR STORY STARTS AGAIN

Maybe you've been reading about good and bad choices in relationships, and you're thinking, *Man, have I blown it big time! Everything I was supposed to do, I didn't. Everything I wasn't supposed to do, I did. What now?*

If so, you're not alone. I often talk with people burdened with shame, guilt, and condemnation. Deep down they wonder, *Can I ever be happy? blessed? fulfilled? How could God love someone who's messed up as big as I have? Does He even still love me? Is there a hope for a better tomorrow?*

If you can relate to these feelings, take a deep breath. It's not too late to begin again.

If you're not a Christ follower, I invite you again to receive the unconditional, transforming love of a good God. As I shared with you in chapter 2, the greatest day of my life was the day I met *the One*—Jesus. And the same thing can happen for you. The fact that you're reading this book is evidence that God is reaching out to you. He loves you exactly as you are. He sent Jesus to reveal His heart for you, to die for you, and to live again. A new beginning in Christ is available to you when you admit you're stuck, turn from your sins, and sincerely call on Him.

In this chapter, I'm thinking especially of those who are stuck in a different way: You have experienced Christ's life but over time have squandered it in a pattern of sinful living. You had great intentions but wound up in the wrong places. What do you do if you've already been born again but feel like you're dying a slow, lonely death?

Maybe it's time to be born again—again.

I'm not suggesting a second salvation experience. Instead I'm suggesting you revisit the love of God as if you're learning about it for the very first time. Examine His grace, not just for the lost who were found, but for the found who wandered and got lost.

No matter how badly you've messed up, your sin is never bigger than God's saving love. Think of it this way: Nothing you can do can make God love you more or love you less. He loves you because He *is* love. And His love for you never changes. He loves you with an everlasting love (see Jeremiah 31:3).

Phil, a successful computer programmer I know, is one of those who found God, only to wander. "I hate to admit it, but

I went through bankruptcy, two divorces, and one rehab before I reached out to God. And I knew better." Phil recounted how he grew up in a Christian home and knew most of the Bible stories, but decided to do life his own way instead of God's.

Phil stood before our church and, through tears, said, "I knew God saved me from my sins when I was a child. I just never expected He'd save me from myself as an adult."

If your life story has been moving in the wrong direction, call on God and let Him write the rest of your story His way. He will. He is a God of new beginnings. His name is Redeemer (see Psalm 19:14). That's what I want to talk about in this chapter.

Serpentine Subversive

One of the ways we set ourselves up to be vulnerable to sin in relationships is that we consistently underestimate what we're up against. Christ followers need to grasp, for example, that we have a spiritual Enemy who wants to destroy everything that matters to God. And *you* matter deeply to God. One of the Evil One's greatest strategies is to trick you into living in shame. Why? Because shame isolates and separates. Once he's got you alone, the rest is easy. He can haunt you at his leisure.

For insight into how the Evil One works, look again at Adam and Eve. Genesis 2:25 says, "The man and his wife were both naked, and they felt no shame." Before sin infected humanity, there was no shame. Imagine that for a moment. No guilt. No hidden skeletons. No fear of being found out. Adam and Eve were intimate with each other, close to God, unburdened. They never said, "Sorry. We blew it." They never needed to.

At least not for a while.

Then the serpent tempted them to sin. When they ate the forbidden fruit and their eyes were opened, the Bible says, "They realized they were naked; so they sewed fig leaves together and *made coverings for themselves.* Then the man and his wife heard the sound of the LORD God as he was walking in the garden in the cool of the day, and *they hid from the LORD*" (Genesis 3:7–8). Our natural response to shame is to cover ourselves and hide. Separation and isolation feel safer. As long as we hide, though, our Father can't clean up our mess, leaving us no choice but to wallow in it.

As parents, Amy and I have cleaned a lot of baby bottoms and our fair share of you know what. During potty training, all our kids had accidents. When they were toddlers, we taught them that "poo poo goes in the potty, not in our pants." Gradually they all caught on. But each kid had another thing in common. They all found their own hiding places when they wanted to sneak away and make little, private deposits. Whenever we'd ask, "Where is so-and-so?" more times than not, our potty-trainee was hiding behind a chair, taking care of business. Why did our children hide? Because they knew what they were doing was wrong. Only when they came out of hiding and faced the truth could we help clean up the mess and restart them toward success.

It's time to let God clean *you* up. Perhaps as you look back over your relationships with the opposite sex, you have to admit that you've used people—purposefully, selfishly, even cruelly. Perhaps you've developed a lifestyle of deceit or lying, or focusing on externals. Maybe you've hung out with the wrong crowd and learned to curse like a character from *The Godfather*. Maybe you became addicted to pleasing people instead of pleasing God. Perhaps your sexual past or present haunts you. Perhaps you had an abortion. Maybe you've been molested and feel dirty—even though intellectually you know it wasn't your fault. Or maybe you've let yourself go and you're ashamed of how you look.

Whatever you're ashamed of, simply naming what happened is a huge step toward leaving the sin and shame behind, and receiving God's mercy, forgiveness, and healing.

Lightening the Load

If your mess is a result of your own sinful actions, it's time to confess. No more secrets. Deal with your sin in the open. Proverbs 28:13 says, "He who conceals his sins does not prosper, but whoever confesses and renounces them finds mercy." It's time to confess.

This raises the question: to whom do you confess? Scripture teaches us to confess to God first for forgiveness. I love His promise: "If we confess our sins, he is faithful and just and will forgive us our sins and purify us from all unrighteousness" (1 John 1:9). Whatever sin is burdening you, confess it to God now. Go ahead. Do it.

Now here's the good news: God has forgiven you. He really has. Embrace it. You're forgiven. No matter what you've done, in God's heart it's gone. If you're devoted to following Christ, when God sees you, He doesn't see your filth and sinfulness. Instead He sees the righteousness of Jesus. You are forgiven—completely.

But you might be thinking, *Okay, I know God has forgiven me, but something still doesn't feel right.* Now it's time to take it another step. We confess to God for forgiveness, and we confess to God's people for *healing.* James 5:16 says, "Therefore confess your sins to each other and pray for each other so that you may be healed."

Before we continue, let me be absolutely clear about something. Everyone doesn't need to know everything you've done wrong. In fact, most people probably *don't* need to know it. But confessing to a few appropriate people for prayer and accountability can be life-changing. When you confess, make sure it's to someone you trust, someone with your best interests at heart.

Tell a close friend, and ask for prayer. Open up to an accountability partner or spiritual mentor. Whatever sin is dragging you down, deal with it today. The more cleansing you have on this side of marriage, the better off you'll be on the other side.

At twenty, I was struggling to overcome my sexually sinful past. I'd confessed to God and embraced His forgiveness. But only when I finally confessed to a friend did I begin to find complete healing. Every time I'd be tempted, I'd call my friend Braun. He'd pray for me. Encourage me. Remind me that he'd beat the crud out of me if I failed.

Over time, God renewed my mind. What once had been a big struggle faded month by month, preparing me to be more like God and ready to love my spouse.

Outside In

Satan's greatest weapon is deception. If he can convince you of falsehoods, he can keep you from God's truth. Here's how the Dark One wields his weapon of deception.

First you experience something painful. You experiment sexually. Someone betrays your trust and abuses you. You make a decision you regret. Then—here comes the lie—Satan tries to convince you that your *experience* and your *essence* are the same. He tries to connect *what you chose to do* or *what happened to you* with *who you are.* He falsely equates the *external* with the *internal,* your *actions* with your *identity.*

That's the difference between guilt (which is truth-based) and shame (which is lie-based). Guilt deals with external doing. Shame is about internal being.

Guilt says, "I did something bad." Shame says, "I am bad."

Guilt says, "I made a mistake." Shame says, "I am a mistake."

Be honest. Are you internalizing some external hurt or failure? Maybe someone rejected you, but you twisted it and made it your fault. You think, *Because he rejected me, I'm worthless. Because she turned on me, I'm no good.* You think, *I failed* [external], *so I'm a failure* [internal].

If you can relate to this pattern, you're living in shame. Shame separates and isolates, leading to hopeless desperation. *After what I did, God could never bless me. I'm destined to be miserable. I'll never have a good marriage. I'll always be stuck.* The Evil One wants you to believe the lies. He wants you to be a prisoner tormented by your past.

But now receive the truth: You are not what you did. You are not what someone did to you. You are not what happened to you.

You are who Christ says you are.

Finished Past, Beginning Future

To break free from the shame of the past, first recognize that as much as you'd like to, you can't change what happened. What's done is done. No amount of wishing, praying, or hoping will ever change it.

King David knew a thing or two about that. After failing big, he was desperate for a do-over.

You may remember his disastrous plunge into sin. He betrayed his loyal soldier Uriah by committing adultery with Uriah's wife, Bathsheba. As if that wasn't enough, he had Uriah placed on the front line of a battle so he'd be killed.

Lust, selfishness, deceit, betrayal, adultery, *and* murder.

Could it get any more complicated? It could. It did. Bathsheba was pregnant.

Nine months later, the tragedy became a calamity. The baby was born, but God had already told David the boy wouldn't live. While David's little one still drew breath, David broke down. He cried and prayed. And cried and prayed. And cried and prayed some more. But the child died.

Then David got up, took a shower, and went to church. His servants didn't understand how he could shift so quickly from crying to calm. He explained, "While the child was still alive, I fasted and wept. I thought, 'Who knows? The LORD may be gracious to me and let the child live.' But now that he is dead, why should I fast? Can I bring him back again?" (2 Samuel 12:22–23). David came to grips with a hard reality. He couldn't change the past.

Neither can you.

But you can choose to walk forward in the light. If you gossiped, you can apologize, but you can't ever take back the words you said. If you aborted a child, your baby is in heaven—you still have a precious life to live in gratitude to God. If you lost your virginity, you'll never get it back, but you can live in purity and celibacy today. If you were molested—your innocence shattered—that historical fact will never change. You can't make even one choice for the perpetrator, but you can choose the healing that God wants for you.

Because, though your past is fixed, Christ can and will change your future—if you'll let Him. Listen to His promise from Romans 8:28: "And we know that in *all things* God works for the good of those who love him, who have been called according to his purpose." I love the phrase "all things." That includes even the things you wish had never happened. The things you're ashamed of. God can take the past realities the Enemy meant for evil and turn them to your good.

David and Bathsheba's sin was bad. But God, in His mercy, forgave them. He did even more. If you read the genealogy of Christ in Matthew 1, you see a miracle. The adulterous woman Bathsheba and the murdering betrayer David are both listed as links in the bloodline leading to the birth of God's Son. Our heavenly Father took a sinful situation and turned it to good. Amazing.

That's what God did for me. Before I was a Christian, I cheated on every girlfriend I ever had. *Every single one.* After I'd surrendered to Christ, I feared my sins would follow me. *Am I capable of being faithful to one woman? Is it possible for one woman to be faithful to me?* Surely the consequences of my dark past would haunt me for the rest of my life.

But God is good. He's way more good than I was bad. He took my darkest shame, my greatest weakness, and brought out of it my greatest strength. In sixteen years of marriage, I've *never* considered straying. Not once have I questioned Amy's faithfulness. God buried my sin, and from its remains grew something good. He can do the same for you.

God's forgiveness is all-important. If you're able, I encourage you to also apologize to those you've hurt. Ask for their forgiveness. In addition to lightening your own burden, you might change someone's life.

When I cheated on the last girlfriend I betrayed, the experience sent her life into a tailspin. Years passed, and I couldn't shake the guilt. One evening I told Amy about it. She wisely said, "Why don't we pray for God to give you the chance to apologize?" So we did.

I had no clue where this woman even lived. But the very next day—I promise this is absolutely true—we bumped into her in a McDonald's. I nearly dropped dead from shock. Once I was able to use words again, I asked for her forgiveness. She graciously gave it. I've been free from that guilt ever since.

Strength for the Journey

Maybe you've turned over a new leaf. You're ready to abandon the past and embrace God's best for your future. How do you keep from flipping back to one of those old chapters?

Chances are, your spiritual Enemy will give you plenty of opportunities to go back. Mark it on your calendar—temptation is coming. But you can be prepared. Let's talk about how today's good intentions can become tomorrow's obedience and blessings.

Go Public

First, it always helps to go public with your new commitment. If you're changing the way you live, let the world know. Not only will your public declaration trigger supportive prayers from other believers, but it will also bring built-in accountability for your newfound direction.

I'll never forget when twenty-year-old Lisa surrendered her life to Christ. She confessed to meth addiction and checked herself into rehab. Overwhelmed by God's love, Lisa wanted to tell her story to our church—thousands of people. I remember hesitating, not wanting to put too much pressure on a new believer. *What if she fails and goes back to meth?*

She pleaded with me, assuring me that she was different, and explained how telling her story would burn the bridge back to her dangerous past. After praying about it, I gave her the chance. Not only did dozens of others come forward confessing their addictions, but Lisa continues to be an example of hope. She'll tell you today that part of her strength is a result of her public confession. Every time I see her at church, she tells me the exact number of days she's been free.

Break Away

Second, you'll want to break free from any dangerous relationships. This is one of the most important steps to living in freedom. Many people, not wanting to hurt or abandon their friends, continue to hang out with the wrong crowd, getting sucked back into the lifestyle they just escaped.

The woman in the previous story, Lisa, is a good example of this principle. When she went public with her new life, she explained clearly that she couldn't spend time with *any* meth users. Period.

Shane, on the other hand, didn't follow this principle. Shane was an up-and-comer with a large company. His sales buddies lived fast and hard—and Shane was smack dab in the middle of a destructive life. A cute female co-worker invited Shane to visit her small-group Bible study. More interested in the girl than the Bible, Shane agreed. He later explained that it was like he walked into a world of love he'd never dreamed possible. On the second week, Shane committed his life to Christ.

All his co-workers were stunned. Instead of visiting strip clubs over lunch or hitting bars, Shane wanted to read his Bible. He was a different person.

But after a while, Shane's conviction started to waver. He didn't want to be a prude and got tired of his friends' ribbing. Torn between abandoning his new life and wanting to fit in, Shane went to a party with his old buddies. Temptation struck. Shane caved. One drink led to two. Two led to too many. Almost without a fight, Shane slipped back into destructive living.

Committing to Christ doesn't mean we rudely dump the wrong friends. Neither does it mean that we suddenly devalue them as people. But we must be willing to radically redefine those relationships if we are to protect our new life.

Get Back in the Saddle

But what do you do if you *do* fail again? You made a great start, you began to establish a solid track record, and then you blew it. You should know better by now, so you're harder on yourself than ever. You're so ashamed that you don't feel worthy of going back to God again. It's the *again* that haunts you. It never should've happened. You thought you were finally past your past.

What do you do?

This might sound too simple. Or it might sound impossible. But if you fall down, God wants you to get back up—immediately. So many people don't. They let Satan keep them down. You won't.

I talked to my friend Randy this week. He reminded me of an e-mail he sent me two and a half years ago describing his painful addiction to pornography. Randy had agonized in guilt and shame for years. He loved Jesus. He also loved porn.

At the time, I suggested to Randy a counselor who specialized in sexual addictions. Randy told me this week that he is *finally* experiencing freedom from his pornographic prison. He explained that he fell back hundreds of times but never gave up. With the prayers of his wife and accountability from two trusted friends, Randy was climbing out of the muck and mire.

If you slip back into whatever used to have hold of you (or even into something new), get back up. Whether you fall once, twice, or hundreds of times, don't stay down. The moment you feel most unworthy of God's love is the moment you need it most. His unconditional love will never be more real than when you don't deserve it. Run to Him. Confess...again.

Failure never has to be final. Have hope. Christ's power pulled you up before. He will pull you up again.

Crises of Two Christ Followers

When you're down to nothing, God is up to something. Your Enemy wants shame to paralyze you, but God wants to use your past to prepare you for a better future. Let's finish this chapter with parallel stories of two guys, both from the Bible, who illustrate both outcomes. Two men who committed basically the same horrible sin—betraying Jesus.

Judas turned Jesus over to the Roman soldiers. When shame tracked Judas down, he bought the lie. He equated what he'd done with who he was. Judas saw no hope. He couldn't live with himself a moment longer, and in self-hatred he took his own life (see Matthew 27:3–5).

Peter's sin was similar. He betrayed Jesus by denying Him when he should've boldly proclaimed loyalty. And he *tripled* his guilt, denying his Master three times (see Matthew 26:69–75). Thankfully, instead of internalizing his outward actions, Peter was deeply grieved by his sin, then later met Jesus face to face.

What did Jesus do? He forgave Peter. And more! Just a few weeks later, He empowered Peter to preach with supernatural effectiveness and lead three thousand people to follow Jesus as Lord…*in a single day.* From God's perspective, it makes sense. *No one* was better qualified to preach the love and forgiveness of Jesus than one who'd experienced it firsthand (see Acts 2).

Two men. Similar offenses. Two dramatically different results. If you're still hanging on to shame, it's time to let it go.

Tell Him about your hurt, your sin, your shame. Confess openly. Cry if you feel like it. Hand Him all the junk from your past. No matter how stained it is, "Though your sins are like scarlet, they shall be as white as snow" (Isaiah 1:18).

God can work in all things to bring about good (see Romans 8:28). And He wants to do it for you.

Be free. Be forgiven. Be healed. And watch God's story for your life start again.

9

ROOM FOR THE BIG ROCKS

A college professor stood before his class and said, "Even if you don't get anything else from my course, I want you to get this." He placed a glass jar on his lectern. Inside the jar he placed four large rocks. The rocks took up most of the space. The professor stepped back, clasped his hands, and asked, "Is this jar full?"

Most students answered yes.

The professor shook his head with mock sorrow. From behind the lectern he produced a pitcher of gravel, pouring it over and around the rocks until the gravel reached the rim of the jar. Again he asked, "Is this jar full?"

Some said yes. Others hesitated.

The professor smiled. "If you're waiting, you're wise." Then he produced a pitcher of water, pouring it into the jar until it covered the rocks and the gravel.

"Is the jar full now?" he asked.

Everyone agreed that the jar was finally full.

"Life's a lot like what you just saw," the professor declared. "With that in mind, what's the moral of this lesson?"

One student spoke up. "You can always squeeze more into your life if you try hard enough."

The professor unsmiled. "Actually, I was thinking the opposite. I think the moral is, *No matter how hard you try, you'll never be able to squeeze in the big rocks...unless you put them in first.*"

Marriage is like that. We all fill our lives to the brim with *something.* Many things, actually. And if we don't put what matters most into our lives *first,* the lesser priorities take up all the room. Later, we'll wish we'd left room for the big rocks. That's why a couple who wants to go all the way in their marriage together must decide what the big rocks are and put them in first.

If you've read this far in *Going All the Way,* there's a good chance that putting first things first is exactly what you want to do. You've seen who your One really is and made a commitment to putting Jesus first. You've seen how often what we do in pursuit of our Two can actually sabotage what God wants for us. And if you've gotten off course, you've chosen to pull a U-turn in your thoughts and actions and start again.

Does this describe where you stand with God?

Then now is the perfect time to commit yourself to—and begin to move toward—the marriage God wants for you.

My New Vow Now

In this and the next two chapters I want to show you three refreshing, anything but "normal," oddly godly relationship principles that help build marriages that go all the way. And each principle is so full of promise for your future that you'd be wise to make all three a part of your life.

Starting today.

In fact, here's a challenge you won't hear from a justice of the peace: make some new marriage vows *now.* Whether you're married or single (even if marriage is years away and you have no idea who your Two will be), these important commitments will lay the groundwork in your life for a supernaturally fulfilling marriage.

Why spend your time and energy practicing intimate relationships that will never go all the way?

These three vows, all from Adam and Eve's story, the first-ever marriage, are based on foundational marriage truths found in Genesis 2:24–25.

I hinted at your first vow in the opening story about making room for the big rocks. This promise addresses our priorities:

Next to Christ, I reserve the priority spot for my spouse.

Earlier, we discussed how to go about finding the One. Order is a universal law: pay attention first to what matters most. The One you're really looking for is Jesus Christ. Find Him first. Earlier I gave you some real-life advice from God's Word on how to find your Two—the person you want to be married to until death do you part.

I want to return to the principle of order or priority, but this time to show why it's so important in building a healthy marriage. Because even after you've found the One and your Two, order still matters.

Harder Than It Looks

"God first. My spouse second."

Doesn't sound like a love lyric from Top 40 radio, does it? Yet "my One first, then my Two" reflects God's heart from the beginning.

God created everything and said it was good—except that man was alone. (Just imagine how grungy Adam must have let his shower get. And forget about picking up after all the animals.) God put Adam into a deep sleep and removed one of his ribs. From the rib God formed Adam's life partner, Eve.

The Bible says, "For this reason a man will *leave* his father and mother and be united to his wife, and they will become one flesh" (Genesis 2:24). When you commit to your Two in marriage, you leave your father and mother. You continue to honor your parents, but your priorities change. *Azab*, the Hebrew word translated "leave," means "to loosen or relinquish." You "loosen" your focus on your parents (or any other priority people), and cleave to your new priority—your spouse. (*Cleave* means "stick to," and cleaving is fun!) Next to Christ—above everything else—your spouse becomes your priority.

You might say, "Of course my spouse will be my priority." But I'll tell you right now, it might be harder than you think.

Consider this: what does Scripture tell us we should give our lives for? You might come up with several noble answers, but among them God does not include money, power, a nice home, or your career. Heck, we're not even supposed to give our lives for an HDTV!

But just one line down on the list, right after giving all of ourselves to our Savior, the married Christ follower is to give everything to his or her spouse. This is true for men and women, though the Bible states it especially clearly for men: "Husbands, love your wives, just as Christ loved the church and gave himself up for her" (Ephesians 5:25). Men, when you become a husband, it'll be an honor to give yourself up for your wife.

There's no question, then, what two big rocks a man should fill his marriage with first:

1. Jesus
2. his wife

And for women, the same principle applies. When God blesses you with a husband, you'll enjoy the privilege of placing him above all others...except Christ.

From Good to Bad

A strong marriage requires the right priorities. What matters most has to come first. Because the truth is, it's not always the bad things that ruin marriages. Often even the good things, placed too high on the priority list, can do damage.

Let that sink in. *The things that destroy marriages are not always bad things, but often misprioritized good things.*

Wait! How can something *good* be *bad*? Simple: the good gets in the way of the best.

How about children? You'll likely never find a bigger blessing than children. We've been blessed with six! But if I neglect my highest priorities and put my children first—before God and before my wife—my disordered living could become very bad for everyone involved.

Your eyes might be shooting daggers at me. *How could you possibly say children aren't important?*

Please don't misunderstand. My children are one of the most important parts of my life. But I won't do them any favors if I give them the place that belongs to my One or my Two. Putting children first feels natural and right, doesn't it? No wonder many parents do exactly that.

But you won't find that children should come either first or second in a marriage anywhere in the Bible. And based on my observation, it doesn't work anyway. If you want to raise an insecure child, put her first, neglect your marriage, fight with her other parent, and let her worry that you might divorce. The recipe for a secure child? Honor God at all times. Love your spouse—and let the child see your affection. Pray together. Communicate. Date. And your child will rest well knowing that Mom and Dad's marriage is strong.

What about friends? They're vitally important, but not more important than your spouse. Many people confide in their friends as substitutes for their spouses, developing those relationships *instead of* their marriages.

How about career? Succeeding on the job is obviously good. But it's easy for a married person to think, *I'm working long hours to help my family get ahead. One day I'll slow down. Then I'll start spending time with them.* But "one day" never comes. Then finally "another day" arrives—the day you look back to see that your spouse is a stranger and your children grew up—without you.

Sure, everyone has seasons when an important lower priority takes a disproportionate amount of time. Maybe one spouse just started a business and has to work long hours to keep it afloat. Or the couple has twins and has to pull twenty-hour days to keep up with them. Maybe they both work while one completes a degree, or one takes a job in a new city and they have to live apart while selling their home. Those are seasons anyone can endure...if they don't become a way of life.

As a newlywed and a pastor, I learned the hard way. Though I claimed that Christ and Amy were my priorities, truthfully I invested my best in my job. I loved the church and worked at least seventy hours a week. When Amy gave birth to our first child, I didn't even drive her home from the hospital. Why? I was working at the church. (Can you say S-T-U-P-I-D?) I *seriously* needed to rearrange my priorities.

If your priorities are out of whack, you can survive for a while, hobbling along, pretending things will get better. But they won't...unless you make a change.

That's what I did thirteen years ago. Just the other day I asked Amy, "Next to Christ, do you feel like you're my priority?" To my delight, she threw her arms around my neck, pulled me close, gave me a big kiss, and told me she was the luckiest wife who ever lived. (I was smart enough not to tell her she was right.)

I'm learning to keep the good things from taking priority over the best.

From Bad to Worse

That said, let's also acknowledge that bad things can break up marriages too. When I say bad things, I don't mean misplaced priorities that belong lower on the list. I mean things that shouldn't be *anywhere* on the list...or in your life. Things like selfishness, too much debt, affairs, pornography, a critical heart, abuse, neglect, and more.

While the destructiveness of those things becomes most obvious in marriage, the seeds are often planted long before.

They may show up as "marriage problems," but in reality they're merely symptoms of the actual problem—a heart warped by walking down a dark and dangerous path.

Before marriage we value our independence. We like to think we're masters of our own lives. Our "little" indiscretions seem reasonably safe. Anger, lust, arrogance, runaway debt... We think:

This indulgence won't affect my future marriage.

I'll stop when I get married.

I'm not hurting anyone today.

What's the big deal?

But "little" problems *before* marriage inevitably result in big problems *in* marriage. They often act like a negative balance accumulating compound interest, and filing for a Chapter 13 marriage starts to look like an option. That's why we need to make and keep our first promise—aligning our priorities to God's—*today.*

Are you letting alcohol, smoking, or drugs rule you? What makes you think they'll just let you go when you're married? Those substances won't respect the priority of your spouse. The wounds you inflict on your own heart now with pornography or other sexual sins won't heal the instant you say "I do." And that habit of overspending won't disappear overnight when you cross the magical border between singleness and matrimony.

Get clean and get healthy now—physically, emotionally, spiritually. Dig the fossilized sins out of the jar, and give your One His rightful place.

Priority Makes Perfect

Marriage may seem a far-future prospect, or it may be just around the corner. Either way, you can put the principle of priority to work in your life *now.*

Here are two practical steps:

Practice the Priorities

Jesus said in Luke 6:47–48: "He…who comes to me and hears my words and puts them into *practice*…is like a man building a house, who dug down deep and laid the foundation on rock." The words He chooses imply we are to *keep learning and applying* God's teachings. That's how obedience becomes a habit.

"Practice makes perfect." It's not just a cliché; it's true.

It's something you can start doing now. In the priority promise, God is always first. Then how about your family? Are you honoring your parents? Are you loving and caring for those in need around you? Are you living with integrity? Are you taking opportunities God sends to tell others about the incredible sacrifice of Jesus?

A marriage that's going to last isn't based on a one-time decision to put God first and spouse second. It requires a commitment that you affirm daily.

For example, when you first marry, you'll be blending schedules and commitments. Add a kid (or six), church activities, work, and hobbies while trying to keep your house up, and before long you're swamped with busyness. Hopefully long before your life is unmanageable, you'll work hard to structure it around your priorities.

What does that look like? You might make a habit of saying no to one invitation or optional activity each week and spend that time together. You might designate two nights a week that are—*Gasp!*—"no TV nights." You might budget a small percentage of your income for some activity you commit to do together.

Practicing the priorities isn't easy. But just like a physical workout, it's worthwhile. And it'll get easier—and immensely fulfilling—as you and your spouse grow stronger.

Protect the Priorities

One important exercise for a couple in engagement and early marriage is to ask, *What priorities will be most important for us throughout our marriage?* Name your marital priorities ahead of time to guide your choices throughout marriage. And don't just talk about them; write them down, and review them together often.

Some couples might choose a priority of uninterrupted conversation time without children butting in. Or maybe spiritual time with other adults. Or completing home improvement projects together. It could be playing games, planning for the future, or parking on a dirt road and making out. Or an occasional weekend getaway.

For Amy and me, getting out of town alone is important. We also limit our social activities. And we have to be very careful not to let e-mail, the Internet, and cell phones rob our attention from what matters more.

We live in an age when guarding priorities is a bigger challenge than ever. Distractions, options, opportunities, and temptations fly at us from every direction. If we want to keep our lives and marriage in order, we need to know what really matters—and then be willing to work hard for it.

Otherwise your jar will fill with gravel, sand, and water first...and there'll be no room left for the big rocks.

Lesson of a Dyslexic Pastor

When I performed my first wedding, I typed the whole ceremony beforehand. Standing before the bride, groom, and hundreds of people, I came to a paraphrased statement from Matthew 19:5: "The two will be united." That's what it was supposed to say. I had accidentally typed, "The two will be *untied*."

Oops.

After the ceremony, I looked closely at the word. Only one small letter was out of place: the *I*.

That's really how it works—when the *I* is in the proper place, submitted to Christ, His will, and His priorities, we'll be united. When the *I* is in the wrong place, we'll be untied.

A spouse that allows anything to take a front seat to God or their partner or both... only goes partway. But a marriage that keeps God, spouse, and self in right order… goes the distance. When God gives you His best—your Two—give your spouse your best. Make and keep the priority promise.

It's worth it. *God and your spouse* are worth it.

10

PASSION AND PURSUIT

Have you ever made a fool of yourself in the name of love? Boy, I have. While Amy and I were dating, she told me she loved the name Joy. I started to dream of the future I hoped would be. *Maybe when we we're married, we could name one of our kids Joy.* (In fact, we did.)

One January, while in Wal-Mart, I saw a latch-hook rug kit on sale for 75 percent off. I knew instantly it was the perfect gift for Amy. Emblazoned across it was the word *Joy.*

Behold, what a wondrous marvel the Lord hath provided! I thought. *A gift of the heart wherewith to spoil my love muffin. And 75 percent off! God is good.* (Didn't you know pastors think in King James's English?)

I purchased the kit and spent the next day trying to figure out how the heck to make a latch-hook rug. I devoted the entire week to weaving three thousand red, green, and white yarn pieces through tiny squares—all in the name of love.

I waited until Valentine's Day to offer Amy my masterpiece. But her reaction wasn't quite what I was expecting. She was trying her best to look appreciative, but mostly she just looked blank.

Shocked she wasn't beside herself with...well...*joy*, I finally asked, "Don't you love it?"

She smiled sweetly. "Of course. Thanks so much for the *Christmas* rug."

Suddenly I realized—for the first time—why the rug had been on clearance in January. The hollies around the edge should've clued me in. I just completely missed it. Thanks to love, my passionate pursuit of Amy wasn't a complete bust: once she realized the meaning behind my latch-hooking madness, she told me it was one of the sweetest things anyone had ever done for her.

People do foolish and wonderful things in the heat of pursuit. But most couples tend to pursue each other more *before* marriage than after. Once married, the couples' passions often cool (sometimes to subzero temperatures). Expectations change. Things settle into a routine. And the chase becomes more of a lounge.

Why?

Because we tend to pursue only what we don't have.

Not Trivial, But Passionate, Pursuit

Not long ago, I decided to purchase a video camera. I read *Consumer Reports*, researched cameras on the Internet, searched eBay, shopped at four stores, then made my kill. But now that I have the camera and the pursuit is over, I've lost interest. It's still sitting in the box. I haven't even used it. I put all that effort into the conquest, then didn't follow through.

Too often that's what happens in marriage.

Guys are especially goal oriented. A man will set a goal and attack it. Once the goal's accomplished, by nature he tends to move to the next goal. The same is true in relationships. Once he catches the girl...mission accomplished! In the words of Larry the Cable Guy, "GIT-R-DONE!" Then he generally moves to the next unconquered goal. After marriage, the focus of the single-guy-turned-husband often shifts to attacking a career goal. It's not that he no longer loves his bride; he does. But in his mind, he's already won her heart. Now he needs to win something else.

What he doesn't realize is that without active, continued pursuit, what's been won can be lost! He needs to establish the habit of winning his wife anew every day.

One of my marriage mentors, Dan, is a great example. He explained to me that every day he commits to do something for his wife. At first, that sounded easy to me, until I actually tried it. Just like he reads his Bible daily, pursuing God, Dan makes pursuing his wife a priority.

His wife, Dawn, described with pride what it's like in a typical week to be on the receiving end of a very wise man's pursuit. Dan sends love e-mails, calls for no reason, comes home early to surprise her, buys her inexpensive yet thoughtful gifts, picks flowers for her, massages her feet, compliments her meals, laughs at her jokes, takes her on dates, reads to her, and notices anything new she does to her hair. The look on Dawn's face as she told me this clearly communicated the value of continued pursuit. She exuded contentment, confidence, and peace.

What about women? After marriage, it's appropriate for a woman to pursue her husband. But somehow I have a problem encouraging a single woman to pursue a man. Call me old-fashioned, but I honestly think it's God's best for the man to be the pursuer before marriage. Does that mean the single woman is passive in the relationship? Absolutely not! I prefer to think of her as *actively attracting* a man, rather than pursuing him. The wise single girl knows how to gently and appropriately encourage the relationship forward without being the aggressor.

It reminds me of something Amy loves—ballroom dancing. (I'm more of a John Travolta, *Saturday Night Fever* guy.) Just for her, I rented a how-to-ballroom-dance-for-beginning-dummies video. The only maneuver we really mastered was dancing our way out of a corner. But the most important thing we learned was this: it's the man's role to lead. He accomplishes this through body language and by gently pressing his hand on her back. If the man does this well, the woman can easily follow. When the couple works together, the results can be art in motion. When they don't, their dance quickly becomes unenjoyable, uncoordinated, ugly, and maybe even dangerous. (For us, since we're no good, it's more of a modern-abstract art that doesn't make much sense to the average observer.)

He leads with passionate pursuit. She responds, offering encouragement, and following his lead. The dance starts. With God's direction, it's beautiful and romantic.

Okay, maybe you've been "dancing" for a while, but now the steps are beginning to get a little old. Basically, your relationship has fallen flat. You just can't figure out how to recapture the lost romance. Let's revisit your past. What are some of the things that gave you both the flutters early on? Did your story go something like this?

He likes her. He buys her flowers. Opens the car door. Sends her love texts. She loves the attention. Bakes him cookies. Drives across town to have lunch together. Overloads her lips with lipstick and kisses notebook paper as a gift to him. (Which, by the way, is kind of gross.)

The guy does what he does best—he pursues her (and loves the chase). The girl does what she does best—she invites him to pursue (and she loves to be chased).

Then one day, the couple marry. And most of the romance, pursuit, and thoughtful acts quickly vanish.

If you're in love right now, you may think, *That might happen to a lot of other couples, but I'll never stop pursuing my honey-love-bunches.* I hope you don't. But please hear me clearly—most people do. Sustaining the pursuit throughout decades of marriage is a greater challenge (and leads to greater reward!) than most people realize.

Now, before marriage, it's thoroughly appropriate to take passion slowly. But when you're married, all lights should be green. Unfortunately, many married couples act like the lights are red. Instead of pursuing, they stop. No matter how good things are, after marriage every couple is tempted to let up on the relational accelerator, when they really should *floor it!*

Which leads us to the second promise at the foundation of a marriage that goes all the way. In such a marriage, both spouses hold to this vow:

I promise to pursue my spouse unceasingly.

The Man Who Bought His Wife Twice

Lifelong pursuit isn't just great for your marriage—it's the biblical thing to do.

Remember Genesis 2:24? God said, "A man will leave his father and mother and be *united* to his wife." The Hebrew word translated "unite" is *dabaq*, which means "to cling or adhere," but it can also mean "to pursue passionately" or even "to catch."

Dabaq is used several places in the Bible. Here are a few:

> I *follow close* behind you. (Psalm 63:8, NLT)

> They are *joined fast* to one another; they cling together and cannot be parted. (Job 41:17)

> They…*pursued hard after* them. (Judges 20:45, KJV)

You can see that biblical pursuit is not a limited-time event, and it's never done halfheartedly; in marriage it's an ongoing process that should last a lifetime. Do you want a strong marriage? Consider this paraphrase of Genesis 2:24: "A man will leave his father and mother and *passionately pursue his wife for the rest of his life.*" Sounds fun, doesn't it?

It *can* be, but it's the kind of fun that'll take some work.

Does that sound contradictory? How can fun be work? Believe it or not, *passion in marriage is likely to fizzle unless you actively and intentionally nurture it.* When a married person neglects it, thinking that passion will continue naturally, soon your spouse won't seem quite as attractive; eventually the spouse might seem downright repulsive. And the grass will start to look greener elsewhere. Everyone needs to water his own lawn. Passivity in marriage is disastrous.

One of the greatest Bible stories of lasting pursuit is the story of Jacob and Rachel. Jacob was crazy about Rachel. He asked her father, Laban, for her hand in marriage, and Laban generously said yes…for a small price. *Seven years of hard work.*

Yikes! Many people I know find it hard to pull off a forty-hour workweek!

Jacob didn't blink. "You got it!" he replied, looking for a

shovel so he could get started. Because of his love for Rachel, time passed quickly.

Those seven years gave Laban time to think. His older, less attractive daughter, Leah, wasn't getting any prettier. No one was rushing to claim her. So when Jacob showed up on his wedding day to receive his prize, Laban pulled a little switcheroo and gave away Leah instead of Rachel.

Completely crushed, Jacob protested. So Laban struck another deal. Jacob could have Rachel in exchange for *seven more years of labor.*

Double yikes! (Married to two *sisters*! That's trouble.)

Jacob considered his new father-in-law's offer. The music rose dramatically. Dust devils swirled by. Somewhere a camel burped.

Laban looked Jacob in the eye. "Jacob, deal or no deal?"

Jacob hit the red button. "Deal!"

This time Jacob could have his bride at the *beginning* of the seven additional years, rather than waiting until the end. After being tricked by his father-in-law, Jacob must've thought seriously about taking both of his new wives and heading for the Jerusalem Ritz-Carlton without serving the second seven-year "sentence." (I would have.) But Genesis 29:30 says that Jacob "worked for Laban another seven years."

Jacob continued to work for Rachel even after he had her. What a concept!

That's what everyone must do in marriage. Continue to work for—to pursue—the spouse who has already been won.

Passion or Preoccupation?

As I worked on this chapter, I asked Amy, "Do you honestly believe I pursue you always?"

I remembered her enthusiastic response when I asked her if I treated her as my priority and expected something like, "Of course you do, sweetheart! You're the best husband in the world. And your muscles are impressive too!"

Instead she said very matter-of-factly, "Not always."

She's right. I occasionally get distracted. Maybe even more than occasionally.

This can happen to any of us. We start with good intentions, but often don't follow through. We decide wholeheartedly in January, *This is the year I'll get out of debt.* And for two weeks we live on a budget and discipline every financial decision. Within a month the good intentions fade, and the debt grows even deeper than before. Or we purchase the *Beach Buns of Steel* fitness DVD, and after two days of rug burns decide to stick with our buns of Jell-O.

When I became a new follower of Christ, my enthusiasm was through the roof. I observed those who'd been Christians for years and seemed to have lost their fire. *I'll never allow that to happen to me,* I promised. But within a few short years my passion was starting to cool.

Relationships are no different. We meet someone and grow to love that person. Even though the romance wilts for most couples, we believe ours will always flourish. Good intentions, poor follow-through. We get lazy. Or distracted. Or bored. Or forgetful. *I intended to—but just didn't do it.*

Flip that picture. When we *do* follow through and pursue, great things happen. Amy and I once saw a couple in their seventies who looked like they had just stepped off *The Love Boat.* He looked into her eyes as they held hands, talking, laughing, wildly enjoying each other. Amy and I couldn't resist asking about their story. They'd been married fifty-one years.

"What's your secret?" Amy asked the wife.

With a big smile, she replied, "He loves me just like when we were dating, only fifty-one years deeper."

Their pursuit never ended.

A marriage that goes all the way is one that closes the gap between intentions and actions. Both partners are determined to keep the fire hot. Like Jacob, they keep working for what they already have.

Decide right now that you'll do the same.

11

PURE INTIMACY: THE NAKED TRUTH ABOUT GETTING CLOSER

Once upon a real, genuine, historical time, true intimacy just...happened. Like the dew coming down, or the sun rising.

When Adam and Eve first married, the fledgling human race was still untainted. Our forefather and foremother knew nothing yet of guilt. Embarrassment. Shame. Distance. "The man and his wife were both *naked,* and they *felt no shame*" (Genesis 2:25).

It's a lot like my toddler son, Bookie. Once, during our home Bible study, Bookie darted into the middle of our circle of guests...buck naked. Flaunting his little bare body, he shouted, "I'm naaaaaked!" He did a little dance, then scampered from the room.

Everyone burst into laughter. The ladies giggled and said, "He's so cute." The guys laughed like Tim "The Toolman" Taylor and joked about the joys of taking a leak outdoors. Bookie was naked, and it was cute. Even pure. He felt no shame.

Why did we see Bookie's behavior as adorable while the same behavior by an adult would be disgusting and shameful? Because Bookie was a toddler, and innocent.

Adam and Eve knew that innocence. They were naked and not ashamed. They didn't worry about fashion. Adam never thought to himself, *Vertical leaves make me look thinner.* Eve never questioned, *Do these pants make my butt look fat?* They didn't fret about labels, colors, cuts, or styles. There was no such thing as Lacoste, Abercrombie, Polo, Seven, True Religion, American Eagle. They never fought the crowds at a day-after-Thanksgiving sale at the mall. They were naked. Secure. Unashamed.

Without shame, Adam and Eve were able to open up completely to each other, sharing true intimacy. They had no guilt to hide. No fear of being caught or discovered.

Imagine the innocent intimacy of a marriage today that goes all the way, where two people don't have to hide behind masks. Though it's not free from insecurity and distrust, this marriage is a haven from shame or harm. It's a place where two people can be emotionally naked—laid bare—and share a bond that humans can't know again till heaven.

That's one dream that *can* come true. For *you.*

In God's original design, open intimacy was the natural condition for man and woman. After Jesus returns, that's once again the state in which Christ's followers will live. Forever. Between those two historic bookends, there's one more place where God intends us to live in something close to original intimacy—in marriage.

That's why every successful marriage must be founded on yet another promise:

I will do everything possible to deepen intimacy with my spouse.

Where Intimacy Lives (or Dies)

I've heard intimacy explained as "into me see." Scary thought…on the surface. It's a life-changer at its core. For years, like most people, I showed only what I wanted others to see. I trusted hardly anyone. However, God empowered me to trust Amy (although not completely at first). Scared stiff, risking possible rejection, I slowly invited her into my pain, my shame, and my regrets. Instead of pulling back, she loved me even more. And she followed suit. She opened up and told me things no one else knew about her.

The resulting intimacy we've cultivated is hard to describe. Because of it, I *am* secure. I am loved. I'm doing life with my best friend. God wants that for every married couple. But you'll have a hard time letting the real you show up until you confront and overcome some very determined enemies.

What keeps us in hiding?

The Hebrew word for "shame" is *buwsh*, which means "to be ashamed, to be disappointed, to become dry." Above anything, what leads to disappointment and shame? What dries up our love, security, and intimacy? What causes us to flee true vulnerability, yet somehow leaves us no less emotionally and spiritually naked? One word…

Sin.

If your goal is to destroy a relationship, then sin. Most any sin will work. Lie to your best friend. Treat your co-worker harshly. Talk bad about your boss. Become arrogant, prideful, or selfish. Criticize. Nag. Belittle. Put your own needs first.

Sin against another man or woman, or against God, and watch the relationship wither. Sin leads to hurt, brokenness…shame.

Which is the explanation for a vitally important principle: *Wherever sin lives, intimacy dies. And where intimacy lives, sin dies.*

Try this with God. Sin against Him without repentance, and you'll lose intimate fellowship with *the One* who loves you most. Every time. The refreshing flip side is just as true. Draw close to Him. Pursue Him. Enjoy His goodness. And watch your desire to sin diminish. Sure, you'll still be tempted. But the closer you are to Him, the further you'll want to run from sin.

INTIMACY FOR THE IMPERFECT

So, Craig, you're saying marriage can only work for two perfect people?

Certainly not! Amy and I sure aren't. If you're hoping for perfection, you might as well give up now. You'll fail forever if your goal is the perfect spouse.

But marriage is sweet between two people whom God *is perfecting.* People who are growing spiritually and becoming more like Christ. When you're with someone striving for purity, you can slowly drop your guard and become emotionally naked, because this person will have more humility than critical self-righteousness. You can risk inviting him or her into your heart, your hurts, your brokenness. You can prepare to go all the way emotionally. That's when a married couple can start sharing their lives—really sharing. When sin is dying, transparency, vulnerability, and intimacy emerge naturally.

God wants marriage to be characterized by purity and open sharing. Our Enemy, the devil, wants marriage to be filled with dirt, the partners walled up, hiding in the shadows of sin. Satan is a thief; he lives to steal, kill, and destroy (see John 10:10). One of his chief goals is to steal, kill, and destroy relationships, and any doorway into a marriage will do. That's why locking the Enemy completely out is vitally important. Every area of a couple's life counts!

But what if either partner (or both) blows it big time? That couple can still overcome sin and regain intimacy. Where sin dies, intimacy can thrive. God is not only the Savior of people—He's the Assassin of sin.

Now, some people might be tempted to think, *Sure, I get away with some sin; it's really not a big deal.* Spouses might even excuse each other's sin, or partner together in sin, thinking they're not hurting each other. They're dead wrong. Sin will keep a marriage from God's best—from going all the way.

In Galatians 6:7–8, the Bible clearly explains, "Do not be deceived: God cannot be mocked. A man reaps what he sows. The one who sows to please his sinful nature, from that nature will reap destruction." Your spiritual Enemy will lie to you, whispering deceiving thoughts: *What you're doing is no big deal. It won't hurt anyone.*

Maybe you discover that your spouse is involved in some sin like cheating on the taxes, exaggerating business expenses, or viewing porn. You might know it's wrong, but by your silence, you condone it.

Don't be deceived. Sin costs. And any kind of sin you excuse can cost your marriage dearly.

One couple I know found out the hard way. The husband had access to large sums of cash at his job. Occasionally, he pocketed some. At first, his wife objected, until he took her on a nice vacation, bought her new clothes, and hired her a housecleaner.

They both knew it was wrong, but they allowed it to continue. She didn't think it would affect their marriage, but in subtle ways, it did. *If he's deceptive at work, is he deceiving me?*

She started wondering, worrying, even looking for lies. Her suspicion aroused his. Before long, their doubts erupted into explosive fights and accusations.

Their marriage quickly disintegrated. Even as they enjoyed the "lifestyle they'd always wanted" (provided illegally through embezzled funds), the nice things didn't do the trick. She accused him of lying. He accused her of snooping. They yelled. He stormed out. And one day he just didn't come home.

That was the longest night of her life. The next day was even longer. Numbers 32:23 is clear: "Be sure that your sin will find you out." What seemed like a covert blessing quickly became a public disgrace when her husband was arrested for embezzlement. His company prosecuted, and he was sentenced to six years in prison. Now, not only are they broke, but they're divorced.

The Cancer of Concealment

A second enemy of intimacy is *secrets.*

Sin and secrets are related but must be dealt with differently. Sin is the root of the problem. Secrets are the layers of unhealthy self-defense that attempt to hide the sin—and most of us have them. Secrets are a fear-imposed strategy to put up a false front, imagining it will make us safe. The truth is, secrets create extreme vulnerability.

Sometimes, we use secrets to hide our sins. Other times, our strategy is to simply hide some character quality, maybe not even a "wrong" one, but something that embarrasses or shames us. You might be forgetful, clumsy, or unknowledgeable in some area. So you cover it up. Maybe you don't know how to swim, or you're afraid of the dark, or you don't feel spiritually adequate, so you put up a front. You might've been a victim of abuse and believe you'd die if your future spouse knew. It's time to face your secrets.

Eddie and Brooke are a great couple from my old church. In high school, Eddie was exceptionally promiscuous. Brooke remained a virgin until a married college coach lured her into a destructive relationship. When Eddie and Brooke met, they were afraid their secrets would sabotage their relationship. Would Brooke still love Eddie if she knew about his sinful history? Would Eddie leave if he knew Brooke had been with a married man?

God dealt with them both about their secrets at around the same time. To really become one, enjoying a marriage that would go all the way, they had to go all the way—emotionally—revealing their deepest secrets. Their mutual vulnerability strengthened their relationship. Fifteen years later, they're a living example of intimacy.

Melissa and Jason met in summer school and hit it off immediately. They had acres of common ground, and their romance grew quickly. Eleven months after their first date, they got married. But Melissa had some secrets that neither of them suspected would harm their intimacy.

Melissa was nowhere near fat, but she thought she was. For years, she'd struggled with deep feelings of insecurity and inadequacy, especially when it came to her body. At sixteen, after her prom, Melissa came home, ate half a gallon of ice cream, then went in her bathroom, put her fingers in her throat, and threw it all up. That was the beginning of a secret that wouldn't go away.

All through school, Melissa fought bulimia. She might go months without binging and purging. But after a while she'd go back to eating and vomiting multiple times a day. Her senior year, in an effort to keep off the weight, she started smoking. Amazingly, no one in her family knew about these addictions. Not even her new husband.

Though her secrets weren't grossly immoral, they were a source of deep shame. So she hid. She cordoned off a dark corner of her life and denied her husband access.

When Melissa started having serious stomach problems, Jason began to suspect something. One evening he walked in as she was regurgitating her dinner. He was devastated. Not just because of her problem, but because she'd kept it from him. *If she was dishonest about this,* he wondered, *what else is she lying about?* Because Melissa had refused to come clean about her challenges, she now had a new one—a struggling marriage.

After two years of counseling, they're still together. Melissa is finally beating bulimia and smoking, and God has saved their marriage. But she could've avoided years of grief if she'd much earlier understood: secrets destroy real intimacy.

Liberation Theology

What should you do when either sin or secrets have damaged the intimacy in your relationship? In both cases, the solution involves opening up honestly. First to God, then to your spouse. And, if appropriate, to other parties who've been affected by the problem or can help with the solution.

If the revelation involves sin, we call it confession. And God's response (and hopefully your spouse's) is forgiveness.

If the revelation involves a secret that is not sinful, then we call it admitting that you're human. While that requires humility, it doesn't have to involve shame or guilt. It just takes honesty and a willingness to accept help if necessary.

Melissa's revelation uncovered something that was not fundamentally a sin problem. Her binging-and-purging struggle was something she faced as a limited human being with understandable shortcomings. But when she opened up, she also found freedom. Freedom from the burden of the secret. Freedom to get help. Freedom that led to greater intimacy, both with her husband and with God.

Dangers of Distance Running

When I was a kid, my parents always wanted me to play the "quiet game." Whoever spoke first, lost. I thought the game was a blast—never wanting to lose. Now I know my parents were just trying to get me to shut up.

A third dangerous enemy of intimacy is *silence.* We're not just talking about a married couple playing the "quiet game." We're talking about couples who struggle with effective and meaningful communication, which always results in emotional distance.

When I ask dating couples their greatest strength, they usually explain they can talk nonstop for hours. When I ask married couples one area of their marriage that could improve, most say it's their communication—they have a hard time talking. How weird is that?

While dating, most couples make conversation and time together priorities. They work hard to be with each other, preferably alone, just to talk. Because they live in separate places, it takes forethought, planning, even creativity. Their transparent and frequent communication naturally builds a growing sense of intimacy.

In marriage, the couple now lives together. The naive newlyweds often think that because they live at the same address, quality and quantity time will naturally happen. The opposite is generally true. Life happens, and conversations quickly get drowned out by louder distractions. (For example, at dinner tonight Amy tried to tell me a story, but our six kids dominated the conversation. Dinner's over. Now I'm in my office typing. Amy just came in and told me the end of the story—two hours later. Married communication can be challenging.)

Just as a person without oxygen can't breathe, a couple without communication can't thrive. Waning conversation punctures our love tank, and intimacy slowly (or quickly) leaks out.

What happens between lovey-dovey dating chat and chilled, infrequent marriage discussions? There's no simple answer. But I'll make some practical suggestions that can help keep the conversation going long after your wedding day:

1. Practice Until You're Good

Many people just aren't good at communicating. Remember, communication is more than words. It includes actions, tone of voice, facial expressions, and body language. If you bring all the modes of communication to bear in your marriage, you'll boost your intimacy. If you let those tools lie unused, intimacy will wither.

I counseled a young couple, Will and Holly, who were struggling with intimacy in their marriage. I asked Holly to give me a few minutes alone with Will. When she stepped out, I asked how he felt about Holly. He immediately began describing his love for her in creative ways. I invited Holly back and asked him to tell her what he'd just told me. Instantly, his body language changed. He spoke the same words, but his face was expressionless. His voice showed no emotion. His arms were crossed, his body turned slightly away from her.

What had changed? He obviously loved Holly deeply. Why was Will unable to express his feelings? Will had a common challenge. His love was very real, but he was completely unaware of conflicting body language. Because they fought often, his defense system kicked in automatically, posturing himself for protection rather than communicating openly and freely.

We worked on saying loving things with his body, not just his words. A loving touch to match his words…a genuine smile as he talked…eyes locked, engaging the soul… A few simple communication tools, and Will and Holly were singing love songs again.

2. Face Your Fears

Many experience communication challenges because they *fear vulnerability*. You'd think that being transparent while dating would naturally carry over into your marriage. Although it can, often it doesn't. These fears generally originate from our past. Almost all of us have been hurt before, which tends to make us cautious about being vulnerable.

My family lives in the country. Our neighbors regularly feed deer, so we get to see beautiful does and strong bucks almost daily. They've become very comfortable around us. We can get very close…until someone makes a loud noise—then they're long gone.

A marriage is like that. When you feed it (working at good communication), trust and intimacy grow. Over time, you become closer than you imagined possible. You talk openly about your fears, hurts, and dreams. Your spouse listens intently, understandingly, compassionately. Others may not understand you, but one person knows the real you. You are blessed.

But with a few wrong moves—lying, deceiving, speaking harshly, belittling, criticizing, or shutting down—intimacy flees, quickly replaced by fear. What once was so natural can quickly vanish, leaving you wondering if your marriage can ever regain intimacy. It can, but it takes time.

I talked with a middle-aged woman in the lobby after church. Through tears she unloaded mounds of fears and reservations about her husband. She blurted out, "I'm so scared. He might hurt me again. I'm not safe with him. I feel vulnerable all the time. What am I going to do if he hurts me again?" She wasn't talking about physical wounds, but emotional ones. Because of his verbal abuse, she didn't feel *emotionally* safe. She wasn't going to open up anytime soon.

Both of them spent months in counseling, hard work, prayer, and sincere commitment before she was able to trust again. Little by little, she began to feel safe. As her husband learned to reassure her, she slowly opened up and let him back into her heart. Decide today that you'll fight with everything in you to protect your future spouse's heart and to remain open at all costs.

Great communication takes hard work. There are no shortcuts. Those things that come naturally before your marriage are often the things that require the most dedication within it. Work at it. Read some good books. Get counseling. Find a mentor. Listen to instructive teaching. You'll never find a bigger relational return on investment than working hard at growing communication.

Love in the Driver's Seat

If you struggle to find and sustain healthy closeness in relationships while you're single, intimacy is not likely to suddenly come easily once you're married. As we've seen in this chapter, authentic intimacy flourishes naturally where its enemies—sin, secrets, and silence—have been declared uninvited guests.

So what could you do today to prepare for an intimate marriage in your future? Ask yourself a few important questions, and then act on your answers:

- How's it going in my relationships today? Am I allowing sin to break honest fellowship with family, friends, co-workers? If so, in what ways?
- Do my current relationships help nurture God-honoring closeness and starve my natural desires to sin? If not, what do I need to change?
- What destructive secrets do I need to get out in the open and turn away from with the help of God and others?
- What mature Christ follower knows me...*really*?
- Who could help me learn important communication skills during this season of my life, and am I willing to accept help?
- Is God trying to tell me anything in this area that I've been ignoring?

God didn't create you to live inside a safe, comfortable, sterile shell. He created you for authentic, growing closeness with others—especially others in the family of God. God Himself desires an intimate relationship with you. And as you know His love, He will send you relationships to share His love—maybe even marriage. In all your relationships, God can help you overcome each of the three intimacy enemies—sin, secrets, and silence.

In my experience, God's greatest weapon in this wonderful adventure is always His own love—a love we find most clearly lived out in the person of Jesus Christ. Have you fully opened up your cautious heart and imperfect life to His love today? In 1 John 4:18, God reminds us, "There is no fear in love. But perfect love drives out fear."

Let the love of Christ fill you. Let it drive out fear. For that matter, let it drive out all the other enemies of getting closer to Him and others. Enemies like...

- Distance
- Insensitivity
- Selfishness
- Sin
- Secrets
- Silence

True love at work is the unbeatable ally of intimacy in any relationship, especially the marriage of your dreams. And God is waiting to show you how to live that love.

12

THINKING DIFFERENTLY ABOUT HUSBANDS

In case you haven't noticed, boys and girls are very different. While sharing a bath awhile back, my three-year-old boy noticed a difference between his little sister and himself. Standing in ankle-deep bath water, he looked down at himself and then down at his sister and said enthusiastically, "Hey, I've got an outie, and she's got an innie." He wasn't talking about bellybuttons.

Men and women are different not only physically, but also emotionally, spiritually, and in so many other ways that it's hard to know where to start. For your marriage to go all the way, you *must* embrace the differences, though it is becoming increasingly difficult. Societal pressures constantly push for equality between genders. So much of it is a good thing. For years women haven't been treated fairly. Equal opportunities and pay for both genders are way overdue. But often in the fight, men and women experience some not-so-great by-products, one being the loss of appreciation for their divine differences.

When I married Amy, I expected to encounter some male and female contrasts, but I had *no* idea about the extent. At every turn, we were both shocked to realize just how different we were. Men and women process information differently. We communicate differently. We relate to others differently. We love our children with the same intensity, yet it's different. We approach risks differently. We relate to money differently. We worship in different ways. Our sexual desires differ. What makes us feel secure? Different things. Our abilities? Different again. (Yes, these are generalizations, but they're often true.)

(Side note: As I'm typing this, I'm sitting on a chair in my living room with Amy sitting by me reading a book. I think it's hot in here, so I'm going to try an experiment—just to prove a point. I'm about to tell her I'm hot. Here goes…

Okay, I'm back. And guess what? She's cold and doesn't want me to touch the thermostat. Does that sound familiar at all?)

We're different not only in how we see and do life, but also in our very distinct yet equally important roles in marriage. As you serve the One and love your Two, you must understand your role and at the same time value and appreciate your spouse's role.

I can't overstate the importance of properly understanding

how different you are. You can avoid the vast majority of marital problems by seeing and working with God's divine differences. If you recognize and embrace them, you'll enjoy great blessings in your marriage. But if you ignore them, it could be fatal to your future union. For now we're going to examine the role God intended for a husband. Later, we'll talk about God's role for a wife.

Make sure to read both sections closely. Though I'm going to speak directly to men here and directly to women later, these sections are for everyone. The only way two can become one is for both of you to understand the other's role as well as you do your own. Then you can truly appreciate how God made you to complement one another.

Who You Are

On one of my kids' birthdays, Amy asked me to take a picture of the Winnie the Pooh cake. So I did. When we developed the film, she was shocked to see a picture of the cake.

"How could you?" she asked, fighting back tears.

"How could I *what*?"

Clutching the picture of the Pooh cake, she looked at me as if I was from another planet. "This is a picture of the cake. I wanted a picture of the whole table, with all the decorations."

At that moment, I knew I had her right where I wanted her. Trump card in hand, I blurted, "You told me you wanted a picture of the cake—*not the table!*"

Amy's jaw dropped. "Everyone *knows* that 'take a picture of the cake' means take a picture of the whole table." She sighed. "You are *such* a man."

I wanted to say, "You got that right. And thank you!" But I don't think she was complimenting me.

Okay, men can do some dumb things, but not everything about being a man is bad. God saw enough good in us to give us some daunting responsibilities, the greatest one being to lead our families in loving and worshiping Him. "For the husband is the head of the wife as Christ is the head of the church" (Ephesians 5:23). At its best, this God-given trait of leadership can be used for great good. At its worst, instead of initiating the positive, many men slip into a dangerous and sinful dominance. They become cruel, angry, and abusive.

Maybe that's why preachers tend to beat men up when they preach. Most Father's Day messages are aimed at telling dads how they need to be more involved with their kids and be better husbands. Telling men what they need to do is important, but I'm going to try a different route. Rather than ripping you, I want to remind you who God created you to be. Instead of telling you what you should do, I want to tell you *who you are.* When you know who you are, you'll know what to do.

God's Leading Man

One day a fight broke out between two high school boys just outside my church office window. Within seconds a crowd gathered to watch. Without thinking I dashed outside excitedly screaming, "Fight! Fight!" Moments later I remembered...I'm an adult...and a Christian...and a pastor. My responsibility is to break up a fight, not watch it... When I remembered who I was, I knew what I should do. (So of course I banged their heads together and knocked them both unconscious. Okay, not really.)

Men, God made you leaders. That's not what you do; it's who you are. Look at Ephesians 5:23 one more time: "For the husband is the head of the wife as Christ is the head of the church, his body, of which he is the Savior." You are called to be the head. (A character in *My Big Fat Greek Wedding* said the woman is the neck, so she can turn the head any way she wants to. We'll get to that in the next chapter.)

One of the saddest verses in the Bible is Ezekiel 22:30: "I looked for a man among them who would build up the wall and stand before me in the gap on behalf of the land so I would not have to destroy it, but *I found none.*" God was searching for godly men and couldn't find any.

John Wesley said, "Give me one hundred men who love nothing but God and hate nothing but sin, and I will shake the whole world for Christ." You will be that kind of man. And you will impact the world...starting with your own home.

Man was created first. Not because you're better than a woman—but because you're not. (Remember, we didn't do so well on our own. That's why Eve came along.) Men were created first because God hard-wired our brains and bodies to initiate godly leadership. No one has to teach a man to lead—just like you don't have to teach a fish to swim or a tiger to hunt or a bird to fly. (I think you get the point.) It's buried in his DNA. (Sure, we can learn from others and become more effective leaders, but we're already designed to be the spiritual head under Christ.)

You have to remember this. Because forgetting who you are can have some dire consequences. Just look at what happened in the garden when the world's first man let his identity slip his mind.

In Eden, Adam and Eve had it all. An intimate relationship with God. A great marriage to each other. 24/7 nakedness. Complete paradise. And only one rule to follow: eat from any tree you want, except for the tree of the knowledge of good and evil. This first couple only had one commandment—not ten—and they still blew it.

You might know what happened next. The serpent tempted Eve, the fruit looked too good to pass up, and she ate a bite—sinning, leading to what would become known as the fall of mankind.

Here's a question you might not have asked. Since God created man to lead, where was Adam when Eve disobeyed God? Fishing? Golfing? Playing Xbox? You wish. Scripture tells us: "When the woman saw that the fruit of the tree was good for food and pleasing to the eye, and also desirable for gaining wisdom, she took some and ate it. She also gave some to her husband, *who was with her*, and he ate it" (Genesis 3:6).

Where was Adam, the born leader? Right there, with her the entire time. As Eve rebelled against God, he sat by, idly observing, doing nothing to stop it. If I had to name Adam's first sin, I'd call it the sin of *passivity.*

I've often wondered why the heck he didn't tell Eve to stop and step away from the fruit. He could've jumped in like Jackie Chan and knocked the fruit down. Or taken a shovel to the serpent's head. Or at least screamed "Fire!" and run out of the garden, hoping Eve would follow.

Instead, he just stood there watching...doing nothing. One of the biggest temptations every man has is to abdicate his leadership and become dangerously passive.

As men, one of our greatest fears—which we hate to (or simply won't) admit—is that we don't have what it takes. Maybe that's what Adam felt. Maybe he wanted to do something but didn't quite know what to say. Perhaps he doubted himself. Hesitated...for one second too long. Almost acted but didn't. And regretted it for the rest of his life. And we're still living with those consequences today.

That's what many of us do. We have good intentions, but we doubt our abilities. A lot of times we hide this deep insecurity with false overconfidence, an almost cocky, self-sufficient attitude. I've always secretly believed that the most outwardly conceited man is generally also the most insecure.

What if we don't have what it takes? That fear often causes us to let go of our leadership responsibilities and become acquiescent. Men, you are created to lead your wives and children. That's why Satan wants to lure you into passivity.

To be the husband God wants you to be, and to have a marriage that goes all the way, you have to remember who you are and act accordingly. That means leading your family in three important ways: spiritually, financially, and "protectionally." (I know that last one's not technically a word, but just trust me.)

Spiritual Leadership

Ephesians 5:25–27 says, "Husbands, love your wives, just as Christ loved the church and gave himself up for her to make her holy, cleansing her by the washing with water through the word, and to present her to himself as a radiant church, without stain or wrinkle or any other blemish, but holy and blameless."

God's Word doesn't say to love her with an emotional love but with a spiritually leading love. We're called to love our wives as Christ loved the church, cleansing her with the water of God's Word.

Let's start with your future wife. After you've been married for a year (or five or thirty), you'll want to ask, "Is my wife closer to Christ than when we met?" If she's closer, ask yourself a follow-up question. "Is she closer to Him *because of* my influence or *in spite of* it?"

The best way to lead is always by example. Because of women's intuitive nature, in general they often appear more spiritual than men (and in many cases they are). Men who are more concrete thinkers and struggle to express emotion occasionally *appear* less spiritual. Men, don't let these stereotypes limit you. To be the leader of your family, you need to be close to your Father, and you need to let that closeness show. If it's difficult for you to talk about spiritual things, with time and practice, you can excel.

For example, my wife loves to pray together. Honestly, I don't enjoy praying with other people (especially long-winded pray-ers like Amy. Sorry, sweetheart, but you know it's true). I like to get the job done and move on. But just as my wife sacrifices to minister to me, I must give up some things for her. And if praying long-winded prayers is important to her, then I have just two words for her: "Let's pray." (And we'd better start now because this could take awhile.)

Many husbands tell me they don't know how to pray with their wives. I always say, "You can be naked with her but not pray with her?" Then I watch them fall silent. Seriously, if you can have sex with each other, you can talk to God together.

If praying is tough for you, try starting with prayers at mealtime with your friends. This is a good way to build your confidence and overcome some of the awkwardness. And you'll be preparing to pray one day with your wife.

You can also lead your Two spiritually one day by reading God's Word together. So many men I know feel intimidated by the dreaded *d*-word—*devotions.* Wives want their husbands to lead them in a "devotion"—whatever that is. A lot of guys freak out. *How do I lead a devotion?* Read a chapter of the Bible together and talk about it. Or pick a good Christian book and read it together each night—you read to her, she reads to you, or you take turns. Or if that's still too intimidating, watch your favorite pastor on television or on the Internet, and talk about how the message applies to your life. Don't worry about being fancy—just lead.

God doesn't just call you to lead your wife but your whole family. So you'll also be entrusted with leading your children in loving Christ. Beyond a shadow of a doubt, the best way for our kids to see a father in God is for them to see God at work in their father. More than anything else, you need to model your growing relationship with Christ—starting now, even before you're married, even before you're a dad.

As parents, our main priority is to gradually transfer our children's dependence off us and onto God, until they're completely dependent on God. As fathers, we must lead our children spiritually. Deuteronomy 6:6–7 says, "These commandments that I give you today are to be upon your hearts. Impress them on your children. Talk about them when you sit at home and when you walk along the road, when you lie down and when you get up."

When you become a daddy, make it a priority to talk about spiritual things with your kids. In today's language, that verse could read, "Influence your children with God's truth. Talk about God, His Word, and what He's doing in your lives while you drive to school, go to gymnastics, and come home from soccer. Text or e-mail a word of encouragement every time you think to pray for your child. All through the day, teach your children to be constantly aware of God's goodness."

My three oldest girls are e-mailing machines. Every day we e-mail love notes and prayers to each other. Yesterday Catie e-mailed me thirteen times while I was at work. This is one way we connect spiritually and emotionally. Think now about those surprising ways you can connect with your future blessings God calls kids.

However you lead, do it prayerfully and intentionally. By intentionally seeking God for direction today, you're building your relationship with Him and strengthening your spiritual leadership muscles. Lead regularly. Lead intentionally. Lead prayerfully. One day, your Two will beam with gratitude.

Financial Leadership

You're also the provider. God calls you to lead in this way. This certainly doesn't mean your future wife won't contribute financially. It also doesn't mean she won't have a say in where the family money goes. What it does mean is that you will take charge in seeking God to make sure your family is moving in the right direction financially.

Being the provider doesn't mean you have to have a million dollars in the bank, but it does mean you're not slipping down the dangerous slope of debt. Take the lead. Set some goals. Be willing to say, "No, we're not going to buy that just yet." Explain why. (And that may mean saying no to yourself on a regular basis!)

As you lead financially, make sure you know what's important to your wife. For example, my wife loves to give. For years, I was so determined to get out of debt that I limited her giving. I squashed one of her greatest joys. That was a mistake. I should've found other places to cut and given her the joy of expressing her heart through giving.

Know what matters most to your Two and try to plan your finances in a way that blesses her. Maybe she works, and having a housecleaner twice a month would change her life. She may argue that you can't afford it. Bless her by finding a way (not by going into debt, but by creatively cutting elsewhere—taking your lunch to work, for example). Show your love by valuing what she values, all the while working toward the family goals.

"Protectional" Leadership

One time Amy and I were in a rough part of town. A suspicious guy eyed us and started approaching. Immediately I summoned all my tae-kwon-do moves (I was training to be a cage fighter) and prepared to stick my hand into the villain's chest and rip out his beating heart to protect my wife. Convinced this guy was about to draw his weapon, I took the stance. That's when he said, "I think you dropped this," and handed me my wallet.

So he wasn't a bad guy. But I could've taken him...and my wallet wouldn't have been the only thing I dropped—know what I'm saying? As guys, we instinctively want to protect those we love. To protect your future bride from physical harm should come as second nature to you.

God calls you to protect her not only physically, but also emotionally. Don't ever overlook this powerful truth: "[Love] always protects" (1 Corinthians 13:7). Chances are, your girlfriend or wife-to-be has been hurt by men. Perhaps her father was uninvolved or left her when she was growing up. Maybe her last boyfriend cheated on her or said abusive things. Some jerk may have pushed her past her sexual limits, using her and then leaving her with guilt and regret. Chances are very good that some man has hurt her.

Decide that you never will.

As her leader, you will *lead-her* to emotional security. Leading Amy in this way has been one of my greatest honors. She had been hurt by guys before I came along, which had left her with struggling self-esteem. Although Amy is drop-dead gorgeous, she didn't believe she was attractive. Though she's brilliant, she felt intellectually average at best. And though she's hilariously witty, she didn't like her personality. God called me to love all these good things about her so she could see them for herself.

If God brings you a wounded woman (and most are, just like most men), He will empower you to find His beauty dormant in her heart. Look for it. See what others overlook. Encourage her. Build her up. Lift her high.

As she begins to open up to you, remember that she's trusting you with her heart. Promise God that you'll never hurt it. Ask Him to help you, guide you, and empower you to love her purely.

When He does, she'll offer you a gift. That gift is her trust. And when she trusts you, she'll give her all to you in a way that no man deserves.

But Wait, There's More

In marriage, God made man the leader—we've established that. We've talked about the ways you should lead. But before you get "I'm the leader. Bow to me" T-shirts printed or anything, read this verse: "Submit to one another out of reverence for Christ" (Ephesians 5:21). God's plan of partnership doesn't just include your leadership; it also includes *mutual submission.* The husband and wife, both submitted fully to Christ, also submit to each other.

Now, you may be wondering, *How do I lead my wife and submit to her at the same time?* You only have to look as far as your Savior for the answer. Christ led the church by submitting His own well-being to save her. He gave His life for her. In the same way, you should submit your selfish desires to serve your wife. He came not to be served, but to be the servant of all.

The word *submission* makes some people cringe. To them it implies second-class citizenship under a cruel, authoritarian leader. But in reality, it is one of the most beautiful words in the English language. Jesus submitted to His Father's will. And He asks us to submit to His higher ways for our lives.

This is God's plan. And it's good. Satan has a counterfeit plan. His plan is as bad as God's is good. Your spiritual Enemy offers a cheap substitute. Instead of godly *leadership*, Satan wants couples to compete for *dominance.*

Who's going to be in control? In other words, who will wrongly and sinfully play God? Using Scripture as a weapon, many husbands wrongly try to dominate and control their wives. You may know the type. *It's none of your business. I'm in charge, and I'll call the shots. Don't ask questions, little woman. I tell you what you need to know.* What a jerk.

Women are also often guilty—using their influence to manipulate and control their husbands. Jezebel was the classic example in Scripture. When her husband didn't get her what she wanted, she spoke sarcastically to him, then took control. (See 1 Kings 18 and 19.)

Husbands and wives can fall into the temptation of dominance. When one or both spouses ignore God's plan of partnership, they compete instead of complete. While they should be completing each other, they instead compete for control. And this battle often surfaces in small, seemingly insignificant ways. Who controls the television remote? Who determines how the toothpaste will be used? Squeezed and rolled neatly from the end, or quickly clutched with a fist, from the middle? (We have settled on separate tubes. Now if we could only get separate toilets.)

More often, though, the battle for control becomes dangerous.

You are not taking that job.

You are not spending another dime.

I don't give a rip what you think. This is the way it's going to be.

If you don't like it, you can leave.

If you don't do what I want, I'm leaving.

Are you overbearing? I know I can be. Do you struggle with dominance? I know I do.

It may be helpful to identify those areas you try to control. Maybe it's spending, or time management, or driving. Where do you try to take over? Repent and ask God to forgive you. If you're married, humble yourself. Ask your spouse to forgive you. Don't play God. You're a poor substitute—a counterfeit.

Learn to Be a Lead-Her

Even today, long before you're married, you can begin to develop your God-given role. If you're dating, you can love your girlfriend to emotional security by moving slowly and being honest and truthful. Practice leading today. Lead your friends closer to Christ. Learn to manage your finances, eliminating debt and preparing to offer financial strength. Protect your friends and loved ones. Practice submission too. Sacrifice your own selfish desires so you can serve others. Develop the traits of loyalty and honesty.

And remember this one last principle. God has given you an important leadership role, but before you can be over others in leadership, you must learn to be under authority. Before you try to be over anyone or anything, be sure you are completely under Christ (see Romans 13:1). When you know who you are, you'll know what to do. You are a man, under Christ, empowered to lead.

Now do it.

13

THINKING DIFFERENTLY ABOUT WIVES

Someone told a joke about two lines of men waiting to get into heaven. One line was for men who were controlled by their wives, and the line stretched as far as the eye could see. The other line was for men who were not controlled by their wives. In it stood just one man. St. Peter asked the one man what he was doing in the line. He replied, "I don't know. My wife just told me to shut up and stand over here."

I thought it was a good idea to start with a joke because this is definitely going to be tough material. As a guy, it's easy for me to tell other guys we need to be leaders. That's something guys want to live up to, aspire to. But the other side of the equation is more difficult.

If you read the chapter about husbands, you probably know what's coming next, so let's just get to it. Ephesians 5:22 says, "Wives, submit to your husbands as to the Lord."

Now, you might be getting a little—or maybe a lot—defensive. *Here we go again. Some preacher telling me I need to be barefoot and pregnant, not speak unless spoken to, and live in humble submission to my man.*

That's not what I mean. But I don't blame you for feeling that way.

Honestly, most teaching on submission makes me cringe. It usually sounds more chauvinistic than godly. Besides, I really have a problem even thinking about telling a woman to shut up and submit because I'm married to such a strong, smart, spiritual woman. I don't know what I'd do without Amy's guidance and input. And I don't see my position as leader as a daily dominance. It's a partnership with two people at the table; God has just assigned me the task of setting the tone and direction, but Amy confidently shares her thoughts and opinions because she knows I deeply value what she has to say.

Remember that verse from the last chapter? "Submit to one another out of reverence for Christ" (Ephesians 5:21). I told you that future husbands need to prepare themselves not only to lead, but to submit their selfish desires in order to serve you. As strange as it may sound, even leading requires submission.

Biblical submission just doesn't fit the dictionary definition of the word.

Ultimately, submitting to your husband requires faith. If you trust God, you trust He has a reason for everything He says in His Word—even if you can't completely understand it. And submission is part of God's Word. He tells us He created men and women to fill different roles.

Think about it this way. Accepting the idea of submission goes against most of what we're taught to believe these days. But really, the entire idea of Christianity is counterintuitive. We gain true freedom by submitting to Christ and His commands—how much sense does that make? But if you're a Christian, you know it's true. What once might have seemed like a contradiction now makes perfect sense to you. So think about the roles of husbands and wives in the same way. It may feel counterintuitive, but you'll gain God's best when you follow His will.

The question that always seems to get us into trouble when we're talking about the differences between the God-given roles of men and women is this: "Why did the serpent attack the *woman* first?" People have offered a buffet of possible reasons, a lot of them suggesting that it has something to do with the woman being the "weaker" sex. None of these answers is useful, and many of them are downright unbiblical. So let's stick with the facts. Genesis 3:6 says, "When the woman saw that the fruit of the tree was good for food and pleasing to the eye, and also desirable for gaining wisdom, she took some and ate it. She also gave some to her husband, who was with her, and he ate it." Two things are important to note:

1. The woman ate the fruit first.
2. The man was with her when she disobeyed God.

We've already talked about man's God-given role—to *lead* (Ephesians 5:23). And Scripture reveals that Adam aborted this God-given role. But what about Eve? What did she do wrong? As God calls and equips a man to lead, God blesses the woman to follow and submit—first to God, then to her husband. Guess what Eve didn't do? She didn't submit to God's standard. Instead, just as Adam sinned with passivity, Eve broke God's rule with the sin of rebellion. They both sinned—*at the same time*—just in different ways.

Holy Rebellion

As God directs, one day you'll probably marry. You'll walk down the aisle, cut the cake, smooch for a while beside the chocolate fountain, then duck under a shower of rice. Before you know it, the bliss wears off, you're six months pregnant, and you're in the middle of the grocery store arguing over the price of tuna. And one of your greatest temptations will be to rebel against the God-given direction and leadership from your husband.

Many men have used the principle of submission to oppress women in awful ways. I won't deny that. In the name of spiritual leadership, these men have often been abusive to women. Because of some bad examples, many women want nothing to do with submission. But just because some jerks—who will one day answer to God for their actions—didn't treat women right, doesn't mean God's principle of submission has changed.

In fact, the only way to be successful in life and marriage is to live a life fully submitted to the Savior. A wild horse won't take the rider to the desired destination—until the horse is broken and submits to the master's direction. When a man or a woman is broken and submitted to God, his or her greatest desire is to please the One.

Ladies, when God brings you a man who is wholly surrendered to Him, it will be the joy of your life to submit to his godly love and direction. Rather than a burden, it will be your delight. As your husband loves you as Christ loved His bride, the church, you will enjoy responding to his godly direction.

But there are a lot of ideas about dating you could submit to *now* that would keep you from finding a truly godly man in the future. This is a dangerous type of submission—the kind God would never want for you, because it makes you a servant of the world rather than a servant of Him.

So, yes, you're called by God to submit. But I've got news for you. By submitting, you're simultaneously rebelling.

What?

When you choose to submit to your husband, you're rebelling against popular trends in society. If you think about it, to rebel against one thing is to submit to another, and to submit to one thing is to rebel against another. When Eve rebelled against God, she submitted to the temptation of the serpent.

Had she submitted and followed God's request, she would've rebelled against the temptation of the serpent.

Are you ready for some unusual advice? To one day have the marriage God wants you to have, to find a man who truly will be your spiritual, emotional, and protectional leader, I'm going to challenge you to become rebellious. That's right, rebel—but not against God. I'm asking you to rise up against three common and dangerous lies. You're going to rebel, but it's going to be a holy rebellion, a rebellion that leads to godly submission.

The "I've Gotta Have a Guy" Lie

Do you know a girl who always has to have a boyfriend (or a husband)? Her life is on hold without one. She snags a boyfriend, and life has meaning. They break up, and her world comes crashing down. After the breakup, she rebounds and dates his roommate or his suitemate or his suitemate's cousin or his suitemate's cousin's little brother—just as long as she has *someone* to date. Some girls feel completely incomplete without a guy.

This is probably one of the first things that comes to your mind when you hear me talking about women submitting to their husbands. But really, this kind of dependence has *nothing* to do with godly submission. Relying on your boyfriend or husband for completion is exactly what you cannot do if God is going to be your One. But it's one of the most common traps women can fall into.

I knew a girl like this in college. I call her Bluebird Girl. (Bluebird Girl, if you're reading this, sorry. Your story was just too good to keep to myself.) Bluebird Girl appeared to love Jesus but believed she needed a guy to be satisfied. I had one conversation with her in the cafeteria, then got this note from her the next day.

> Dear Craig,
>
> After our brief conversation at lunch, I prayed for two hours about you. While I was praying, my favorite bird, a bluebird, landed on the windowsill. God was showing me that we're supposed to get married. I know God will confirm it in your heart too. Please let me know how we proceed from here.

I immediately wrote back.

> Dear Bluebird Girl,
>
> Shoot the bird.

Okay, I didn't really do that, but I wanted to. I didn't marry Bluebird Girl. Neither did the next guy she chased. Or the one after that. Instead of becoming whole in her relationship with God, she tried to use God to trap a husband.

Just as the serpent tempted Eve, basically saying, "You aren't complete without the fruit," he'll attempt the same strategy with relationships. "You aren't complete without a guy." And the lie won't stop there.

You aren't really desirable. If you were, you'd be married by now.

Your time is running out.

You're nothing but a third wheel in a two-wheel world.

All the good guys are falling for other girls.

You'll always be miserable without a husband.

Everyone is getting married—but you!

Lies! And you must rebel against them. As long as you believe them, you're setting yourself up for continuous disappointment. No *man* will ever complete you. Only God can. He is your One. And only He can be everything you need.

Scripture teaches this incredible truth: "And my God will meet all your needs according to his glorious riches in Christ Jesus" (Philippians 4:19). This verse is often quoted in reference to physical provision, but its meaning is much broader. God will meet "*all* your needs." Do you have an emotional need? God will meet it. A spiritual need? God will meet it. A relational need? God will meet that too. Whatever your need, a *man* is not your answer; *God* is.

You are complete in Him and Him alone. Remember, single is a whole number. Jesus, the Son of God, never married—and He was more complete than any person who ever lived. He found His total security in His heavenly Father. So can you.

The "I Have to Be Drop-Dead Gorgeous" Lie

This one is tough because your spiritual Enemy will attack you with it at every turn. From the time you're in diapers, you're blasted with messages about external appearances: *Cinderella, Beauty and the Beast, The Little Mermaid.* Models airbrushed to perfection stare you down at the checkout stand. Larger-than-life celebrities glare at you from billboards. Beer commercials filled with perfect bodies (bodies that would never look so good drinking all that beer) invade your television. The heart of the message is: *the pretty girl gets the guy—and you're not her.* But it goes much deeper. Maybe you've believed some other version of this dangerous lie:

You'll never measure up.

You can't compete with all those other girls.

You're not attractive.

You're too fat. (Or too thin. Or too short. Or too tall.)

You're not pretty enough to get a great guy.

I'm not going to pretend for a moment that guys aren't visually oriented because they are. I'm also not going to say that you shouldn't take care of yourself and present yourself well, because you should. But I will argue till the day I die that society puts way too much emphasis on looks. Remember what Scripture says? "Charm is deceptive, and beauty is fleeting; but a woman who fears the LORD is to be praised" (Proverbs 31:30).

Commit this verse to memory. Internalize its meaning. "Charm is deceptive"—it's shallow, not genuine, and doesn't build lasting relationships. "Beauty is fleeting"—here today, gone tomorrow. Gravity takes over. Time always wins. No matter how much a person gets tucked, plumped, or injected, outward beauty is temporary and fading. (Besides, too many plastic surgeries will make you look like an alien. Have you seen Joan Rivers lately?)

But real beauty? A woman who fears God, who is surrendered to His heart and ways, will be praised. King Lemuel asked, "A wife of noble character who can find? She is worth far more than rubies. Her husband has full confidence in her and lacks nothing of value. She brings him good, not harm, all the days of her life" (Proverbs 31:10–12). He continued describing this godly woman:

> She is clothed with strength and dignity;
> she can laugh at the days to come.
> She speaks with wisdom,
> and faithful instruction is on her tongue.
> She watches over the affairs of her household
> and does not eat the bread of idleness.
> Her children arise and call her blessed;
> her husband also, and he praises her:
> "Many women do noble things,
> but you surpass them all." (verses 25–29)

For many men, good looks are the number-one priority in their search for a wife. But those are not the kind of men who will love you as Christ loves the church. A man who is following Christ will search for higher and more lasting values.

God gave me a tremendous gift in Amy. The way He allowed us to meet proved more valuable than I could ever describe. I talked with Amy on the phone before I had any idea about her appearance. We talked and talked and talked—and developed a friendship based on Christ, not physical attraction. I was blessed to first be attracted to her as a person. Honestly, even though I'm very attracted to her physically, it was her heart that drew me close at the beginning.

Do you want to be beautiful? Get to know the Beautiful One—your heavenly Father. There's something about a woman who is secure in Christ. She radiates His love.

First Peter makes this clear:

> Your beauty should not come from outward adornment.... Instead, it should be that of your inner self, the unfading beauty of a gentle and quiet spirit, which is of great worth in God's sight. For this is the way the holy women of the past who put their hope in God used to make themselves beautiful. (3:3–5)

Do you spend more time working on your outward appearance or on inward, lasting qualities? Be honest with yourself. How many hours do you spend reading fashion magazines versus reading God's Word? Do you devote as much time to church as you do to the gym? When preparing for a big date, are you investing as much time in prayer as you do in front of the mirror?

As tempting as it is to focus on fashion, image, your hair, and your figure, don't forget your greatest asset: your heart for God. Seek Him. As you do, He will fill you with His overflowing love. You will be beautiful—in every way—but mostly because God is beautiful in you!

The "I Can Change Him" Lie

If I've seen this once, I've seen it a thousand times. Please don't be number 1,001. A sweet, beautiful, talented, Christ-following girl meets a not-so-great, all-the-lights-are-red guy and thinks to herself, *He might not be great now, but I can change him.*

It's time for a holy rebellion. Rebel against that lie! You can't change anyone—*especially him!*

You might recognize the following scenario.

Sweet Girl meets Jerk Guy. Everyone but Sweet Girl knows Jerk Guy is, well, a jerk. For some reason her friends can't understand, Sweet Girl thinks Jerk Guy is great—or at least *will be* great when she's through with him.

Don't get me wrong, Jerk Guy has some decent qualities. Every now and then, Jerk Guy does something kind of sweet. But everyone who knows him agrees he's mostly a jerk.

Sometimes Jerk Guy pushes Sweet Girl to do things sexually. Other times he tells her she isn't attractive. Jerk Guy often flirts with other girls and is completely into himself.

Everyone knows that Jerk Guy treats Sweet Girl badly. Even Jerk Guy's friends agree that his future isn't that bright. Sweet Girl's parents pray daily that she'll dump him (and even consider applying to be on *Parental Control* on MTV). Her friends all wonder what she sees in him. Little do they know what's going on inside Sweet Girl's mind:

They just don't know him like I do.

He has so much potential.

Everyone who loves me is just plain wrong.

I know he's not perfect, but I can change him.

Sweet Girl, please wake up! If everyone who loves you says you're dating Jerk Guy, you're dating Jerk Guy. Please listen before it's too late! Look at it like this: Imagine you're looking for a car to get you safely to work or school. Would you go to a junkyard and say, "I'm looking for a fixer-upper"? Let's say you find one that has a big dent in the side and hasn't run in over two years. Everyone tells you the car is a pile of junk. You wouldn't say, *They're all wrong. They don't see what I see in this car. Perhaps, with a couple of years of work, I could even have this car running. I want what everyone else says is no good.*

You'd listen to the wisdom of those who love you. You'd continue your search for a car that was in good shape. Why, then, do so many great girls date and marry not-so-great guys? Why would they return again and again—and even say "I do"—to someone who doesn't treat them with respect?

The answers are very complex. If you find that you consistently date guys who don't respect you, consider these options.

Maybe you enjoy a challenge. That can be an admirable trait. But when prayerfully looking for a husband, you don't want a fixer-upper. That doesn't mean the guy God has for you is going to be perfect—that's obviously impossible. And it doesn't mean you won't be drawn to a person who takes some work to attract. You might be, and there's nothing wrong with that. But you want someone who will embrace his role as spiritual leader. You don't want a person whom you have to fight just to keep corralled in God's truth. (If you want a challenge, take up skydiving. It's safer.)

Or maybe you'd argue, "But, Craig, I only attract jerks. No matter what I do, I'm always attracting the wrong kind of guy. Every guy I date is only interested in one thing." If the wrong type of guy is always jumping on your hook, maybe you're fishing with the wrong kind of bait. *Ouch.* Before you get mad and slam down this book, think about it. If every guy who calls only wants sex, maybe you're sending the wrong signals.

So try some different bait—send a message that contradicts the world's heartbeat. Instead of flirting, try genuine friendship. Instead of cleavage, try character. Instead of lying on the bed, try kneeling to pray. Don't be surprised if a very different type of guy shows interest.

Maybe you're seething right now, thinking, *Craig, I don't flirt and wear tight clothes or any of that. How can you say it's my fault I attract these bad guys?* Well, giving off the wrong signals is only one reason you could be drawing the wrong kind of guys to you. Another reason may be your insecurity. Girls who don't like themselves, who feel like they're not good enough to be loved by godly men, often attract guys who are looking to take advantage of them.

To solve this problem, you have to learn to feel confident in who you are in Christ. If your insecurities run deep, get help from a pastor, friend, counselor, or loved one. Spend time with people who care about you and support you. Remind yourself often how worthy you are of real affection and respect. And remember what I said about emotional leadership in the last chapter: a godly man will see the beauty in you and bring it out.

God loves you more than anyone on this planet ever could. So love yourself enough to shrug off the jerks and find a man who will treat you the way you deserve to be treated.

All Three Lies in One

Becca had always been rebellious by nature. When other girls wore dresses, she wore jeans. When the teacher said, "No talking," Becca passed notes. When her parents said to be home by midnight, she'd push the limits, always arriving late.

Becca's rebellion grew—as rebellion typically does. By college, she was drinking regularly, using drugs, and making her way through several guys on the baseball team. One night, she followed the cute second baseman to a Bible study and heard the story of Jesus. This time she rebelled against everything she had been doing and quickly and fully gave her life to the One.

Learning who she was in Christ caused several things to

change quickly. Instead of needing a boyfriend to make her feel secure, Becca found meaning in her relationship with Christ. Instead of putting all her attention on her outward appearance, Becca learned that she was special, not because of her looks, but because of who she was inside. As her confidence grew, so did her standards. Now, not just any "hot guy" was enough for her. She wanted someone who was hot for God—pursuing Him passionately. And she was willing to wait.

Becca rebelled against society's norm. Eventually she met someone equally different. Travis, also rebellious, fought against what most people stood for. He was strong morally, saving himself for marriage, and deeply passionate about leading people to Christ—especially whomever he married. Becca and Travis hit it off immediately but took their time developing their friendship. Nineteen months later, I performed their wedding. That was nine years ago. Today they have three children and are full-time missionaries. Both are completely fulfilled—all because they rebelled.

Transformed, Not Conformed

The devil wants you to conform to the image of this world. But you are rebellious. You're passionate about fighting against his dark lies and submitting to God's righteous ways.

The Bible says in Romans 12:2, "Do not conform any longer to the pattern of this world, but be transformed by the renewing of your mind." When most women settle for the common lies, you're hungry for something different, something better. You crave a godly marriage, under the One and with your Two, submitting to him as God calls you to. And because of that heavenly desire, you'll be rebellious—not conforming—but submitting to the loving, transforming power of your One, Jesus.

14

HABITS OF THE HEART

Did you ever play with a Magic 8 Ball? You know, the black grapefruit-sized ball with the floating triangle inside that supposedly could answer life's toughest questions? I must have asked every version of the question:

"Magic 8 Ball, Magic 8 Ball, will I meet my dream girl?"

It seems like 8 Ball always answered either, "Not Likely" or "Ask Again."

(I hated that stupid ball.)

Like so many people, I wondered, *Who can I find that will make me happy?* It's not a bad question…unless it's the only question you ask as you dream about your future spouse. Here's a more important question, and I'll admit, a more challenging one: *What person do I need to become so I'll be ready for a healthy, fulfilling marriage...and bless my spouse-to-be?*

What kind of person are you looking for? If you had to make a list, what would you write? Surprisingly, most of us would come up with similar lists. Someone who listens, who's kind, who won't hold grudges, whom we can get along with, who won't spend all our money and put us in debt.

Do you think you can be that kind of person for someone else? Are you willing to let God work in your life to grow you in that direction?

Waiting in patient anticipation for the person God has for you isn't the same thing as doing nothing. All through this book, we've talked about the importance of character. Your character is *who you are.* But now I want to focus more on practical life skills—on *what you do.* I call them habits of the heart, and I've stated each of them as first-person commitments because if you make them your own now, you'll realize a huge payoff later in the marriage of your dreams.

Habit 1. "I Will Deal with My Past."

Far too many people carry baggage from their families or from previous relationships into new ones. (Ya got some junk in your trunk—and it's not the good kind.)

Stefan is a great example. After seeing his mom betray his dad with an affair, Stefan lost hope for marriage. Throughout his twenties, skeptical of all women, Stefan hopped in and out of relationships, always stopping short of real commitment. His small group finally talked him into getting Christian counseling. After months of digging into his broken dreams and shattered expectations, his counselors (both the Holy Spirit and the one who charged $150 an hour) helped him heal. Now thirty-six, Stefan has unpacked his baggage and emptied his trunk, and he's enjoying his seventh year of marriage.

No matter how you've been hurt, God can bring healing. Don't wait to inflict the spouse of your dreams with your unfinished business. As much as possible, deal with it now.

What baggage are you carrying? Maybe your parents fought nonstop. Deep down you don't believe a good marriage is possible. You might've been dumped, and now you feel like you're worthless. You may have terminated a pregnancy, or helped someone to do so, and you fear that God will never bless you again. You may feel as if part of you died a long time ago.

Identify your baggage. Seek help, realizing that it may come from a variety of sources. God's Word will renew your mind. Or you might seek advice from your pastor, counselor, or friend. Look for good resources online or at a bookstore. And pray to the Great Physician, Jesus, for healing.

Habit 2. "I Will Grow with Good People."

Many people run headlong into marriage without ever having experienced or sustained any significant long-term, healthy,

God-centered relationships. Maybe you've spent your single years hanging with (partying with, identifying with, sleeping with) people you *know* would make disastrous marriage partners. And yet I can't tell you how many young couples stand at the altar with exactly those scenarios on their marriage-candidate résumés.

Your single years are an irreplaceable opportunity to prepare yourself relationally for a fulfilling and enduring marriage. Make the most of them.

Develop the second habit of love with the commitment: "I will grow with good people."

When I say "good people," by the way, I'm *not* saying you should only spend time with anemic greenhouse saints who spend every weekend fasting and praying in the church basement. What I mean instead is that you should surround yourself—and especially take as your mentors—those people who are obviously of sound character, who encourage you to be honest about your struggles, who love God and put Him first, and who will help you get where you need to go.

A few relationship filters can help you think clearly on this issue. In my book *Chazown*, I suggested four questions that Christ followers should ask regularly to make sure their relationships are contributing to, not preventing, the future they want.

1. **What relationship needs to be initiated?** Is someone mentoring you in important areas—like your spiritual life, your business, your thinking about marriage?

(Even if you're single, find a couple with a strong marriage and hang out with them.) Do you have an accountability or prayer partner? A group of strong Christian friends to do life with? Who's missing from your circle of support? Find them.

2. **What relationship needs to be nurtured?** Have any of your important friendships or family relationships drifted? Are you neglecting someone significant in your life? Learning to nurture existing relationships will prepare you to nurture your marriage.
3. **What relationship needs to be restored?** Is one of your important relationships broken? Maybe you aren't talking to your dad. Perhaps you had a misunderstanding with a best friend. Maybe someone offended you, and you're holding a grudge. Make things right. Do whatever you can, even if it's hard, to make peace (see Romans 12:18).
4. **What relationship needs to be severed?** Is there a relationship that's hurting your connection with God or leading you into danger? Maybe you need to distance yourself. In particular, if you're dating someone you know is not God's best for you, break free. (See chapter 7 for more on breaking up.)

When couples ask, "Craig, do you think we should marry?" I always check into their other relationships. I want to see if both have close, same-sex friends. Have they learned to work through family conflict? I'm excited when they have mentors and accountability relationships. Your working patterns today will make your marriage work tomorrow.

Habit 3. "I Will Learn to Be a Listener."

Without a doubt, one of the most talked about and least practiced habits of love is the art of *listening.*

Does learning how to listen sound meek and mild to you—like learning not to yawn at tea parties, or remembering to sit up straight at Grandma's house? Don't kid yourself. It's huge. Listening well invites love and makes it grow. Listening poorly or not at all kills it slowly.

Next time you're out, do some couple-watching. Some couples barely talk. Instead they stare around the room or pick at their food in near silence. Does each person suddenly have no thoughts or feelings? Has nothing happened worth mentioning to the one person the other cares most about? Certainly not. They haven't run out of things to say. Either one or both have forgotten how to listen.

You might think you're a good listener. Trust me, you'd be the exception. Virtually everyone hears, but few listen. There's a big difference.

I've been incredibly guilty of not listening. When my wife talks, I'm often thinking of something else or busy formulating my answer. Neither action is listening. Sometimes she'll ask, "Did you hear what I just said?" Subconsciously I'll have heard her last four words, and I'll spit them back out. But she knows

I wasn't paying attention, and you can guess how that makes her feel.

Several years ago, I had a consultant analyze my leadership skills. She told me bluntly, "You stink at listening." When I realized she'd just said something important, I asked her to repeat it.

For some, listening comes naturally. If it doesn't for you (like it doesn't for me), practice listening. For example:

- When someone is speaking, stop everything and focus intently on the other person. Don't think about something else. Don't formulate your response (trust me, this one doesn't go over well). You're listening, and your goal is to comprehend not just the person's words, but their heart.
- Don't just listen with your ears, but also with your eyes. Pay attention to facial expressions and to body language. You'll be surprised how much information comes through gestures and stance, even through how the other person breathes while they're talking.
- Repeat back to the person what you're hearing so the other person knows what you heard. By telling Amy what I think she meant, I can confirm that I've understood her. It also affirms to her the value of what she said. As a guy, sometimes it feels like overkill. Not to Amy. It shows Amy not just that I heard her, but that I was listening. Which demonstrates to her that I care.

HABIT 4. "I WILL GUARD MY HEART."

Because you want your marriage to be passionate, intimate, and emotionally rewarding, it only makes sense that you shouldn't wait to get your "heart muscle" in shape for the experience. We all bring different levels of emotional development into a marriage. Some of us grow up in healthy emotional environments and have a head start on heart issues; some of us do not. Those who don't must start from scratch to learn to identify and process feelings (good and bad), to learn a healthy sensitivity to the feelings of others, and so on.

That's why the fourth personal skill I recommend you work on is to guard your heart. Two valuable habits come to mind: developing both a *thick skin* and a *soft heart.* Kind of like M&M's—crunchy on the outside and soft on the inside.

Here's what I mean:

If little things bother you, ask God to thicken your skin. Why? Little offenses and unintended hurts, improperly managed, can accumulate into major woes in marriage. Remember, it's not all about you (hard to believe, I know). When people are rude, it's often more their problem than yours. Are you going to let their bad attitude drown you? Or will you to choose to "duck it"...and let their rain roll off your back? Your response will largely determine your outlook.

For years I was easily offended. If someone didn't say hi to me, I'd think, *Well, who do you think you are? You're nothing but a lowdown, no-good, prideful, cocky punk. I hope you get hemorrhoids before you're thirty.*

Not good.

I have a friend who used to be prone to angry outbursts. He and his wife discussed it, and they agreed that when he did it around her, she would let him know immediately with a key phrase: "Who does your anger affect most?" Of course, his answer always had to be: "Me." So he was able to break the bad habit and the cycle.

I can tell you from years of experience (sorry, Amy) that your future spouse, as wonderful as he or she may be, will drive you crazy at times. Learn today to let the small things go. Your identity is found in Christ; no one's opinion changes that. If you respond with the good kind of thick skin, you'll avoid the temptation to personalize and internalize other people's actions.

But don't let yourself become hard through-and-through. (What kind of M&M's candy would you be then? Like some kind of chocolaty jawbreaker.) While your skin sensitivity is toughening up, allow your heart to soften. Learn compassion for others. Develop the ability to see things from other people's perspectives, to feel for them and with them—a valuable part of intimacy in marriage. The Bible says many times that Jesus was moved with compassion for hurting people (see Matthew 14:14; 15:32; 20:34; Mark 1:41; 6:34). Learn to care so deeply that, like Jesus, you're moved to action.

Through conscious effort, I'm learning to ask, *How might*

this person be feeling? What wounds has he experienced? What would it be like to walk in her shoes? This has dramatically increased my intimacy and rapport in many relationships.

And increased empathy has been one of the greatest blessings in my marriage. At night, Amy and I talk and try to understand what the other has gone through that day. As she talks, I imagine the challenges of homeschooling six kids, making meal after meal, changing diapers, answering calls, caring for sick children. (Just typing those words makes me sweat.) She does the same for me. As we try to feel each other's struggles, our love and compassion grow. Our prayers for each other deepen. And our marriage is always better.

There must be a hundred ways you can make a difference in the lives of the people around you right now. An ounce of compassion provides a lot of refreshment in this world's thirsty relational desert.

Thick skin. Soft heart.

The single years are also the time all of us need to begin cultivating the habit of *forgiveness.* A soft heart definitely makes you more merciful. And believe me, in marriage you'll need it. When you've been wronged—a friend says something behind your back, your parent breaks a promise—don't continue to harbor resentment.

Letting it go is difficult because emotional wounds—like physical wounds—take time to heal. But if you hang on to the grudge, it'll weigh you down and corrode your heart. You need to forgive, if for no other reason than to relieve yourself of a burden. And you need to forgive whether or not the other person apologizes or repents.

Take Matt, for example. He dated a girl who cheated on him. Recognizing her sin, she repented to God and to Matt. But Matt admitted that he hadn't forgiven her. And his grudge kept him from fully trusting people in general. Every time he met a nice girl, he suspected that she, too, might one day betray him. He became a prisoner of his own distrust.

But how can I forgive someone for a massive betrayal? The kind that cuts deep and leaves the most lasting scars?

As impossible as it might seem, we're called to forgive in the same way Christ forgave us (see Colossians 3:13). I've struggled desperately to forgive a few people who betrayed me. Eventually I look at their one offense stacked beside my virtually infinite number of offenses against God. Since He's continued to love and forgive me, surely I can do the same. Christ always changes my heart. But often it takes some time. He'll do the same for you.

Habit 5. "I Will Practice Facing and Resolving Conflict."

Before marriage, I thought healthy couples never fought. But I learned the opposite is true. Marriages are healthy *because* the couple learns to face and work through problems. They fight, but they fight fair. (One time during a fight, Amy came crawling to me on her hands and knees. She told me to come out from under the bed and fight like a man.)

To be prepared for your Two, you need to learn to *resolve conflict.* The first step to resolution is *not* to avoid it, which is what most of us try to do. Why? Because arguments are awkward and make us feel bad. Or we think good Christians shouldn't experience them. But like unresolved hurts and poor listening habits, letting avoided and unresolved conflicts pile up in a relationship will eventually snuff out the love.

If someone on my staff is underperforming, correcting the person will be awkward but could lead to improvement. If I'm always late, it might be awkward to confront me, but at least I'll have to deal with what my tardiness inflicts on others, and in the future I'm more likely to be on time. Similarly, in your future marriage, awkwardness is not something to run from but something to embrace. Conflict is unavoidable in marriage. (But you won't need to go looking for it. It will come to you.)

Here are a few simple conflict guidelines to practice before you say "I do":

- **Don't yell, scream, or throw plates.** Determine that you'll never fight when you're angry. Count to ten (or a hundred) before you respond. When you're angry, you'll say things you regret. Train yourself not to respond in anger. Respond with love. Or at least with calm.
- **Never go to bed angry.** The Bible teaches us to not let the sun go down on our anger (see Ephesians 4:26–27).

I thought this verse applied only to married couples, but it's for all relationships. If your friend, co-worker, or parent angers you, make it right before ending the day. Don't give the devil a foothold in your relationship.

- **Never get historical.** Did you wonder if I intended to write "hysterical"? Actually, I didn't. I meant *historical.* Don't bring up the past. A sure way to damage the future is to dig up ancient ammo. Leave old hurts buried.
- **Never say *never* and *always.*** When you're fighting, it's tempting to exaggerate for emphasis. "You *never* compliment me." "I *always* build you up." Those statements simply aren't true. Avoid extreme words, unless you want extreme fights.

Think of these as the Geneva Convention rules for enduring relationships. Develop them as habits of your heart now with friends and family, and you'll be in much better shape to contend for a healthy marriage.

HABIT 6. "I WILL BE FINANCIALLY RESPONSIBLE."

You've probably heard people say that money problems are one of the most common reasons for conflict in marriage and for divorce. But what you don't hear is how easy it is to trace those money problems to irresponsibility, laziness, and just plain ignorance about money management in the single years.

Do we really think that after years of being careless about

personal finances or alienating friends because we're not responsible housemates, we'll suddenly turn wise when we have two people to think about? Wisely managing God's resources is one of the most important habits you can learn for marriage.

Let's start with the basics. If you're in debt, you're in bondage. Proverbs 22:7 says, "The borrower is servant to the lender." The Hebrew word translated as "servant" can also be translated "slave." If you're in debt, you have an unfeeling master, and you're certainly not free. No matter how frugally you have to live now, make these years count by learning to save and tithe (that's 10 percent), and by managing your bills sensibly.

And don't wait until some time in the future to stay out of—or get out of—debt. If you're married and in debt, you're vulnerable to money fights. On the other hand, if you're a servant to no one but Christ—that is, among other things, you have no debt—it's impossible to describe the freedom this brings to marriage.

Thankfully, when Amy and I married, our only debt was our mortgage. We decided to live a radically simple lifestyle. We never bought new clothes, didn't exchange birthday or Christmas gifts, drove ancient cars, and ate out only with buy-one-get-one-free coupons. As a result of our very countercultural lifestyle, we paid off our inexpensive home in five years. In our late twenties, we were 100 percent debt free. Now, as a team, we're unhindered by debt pressures, and we're free to use God's resources for great good.

You can experience this, too, if you start now. If you have

debt, get crazy about paying it off. If you're debt free, make a promise to stay that way, living only on what you make.

While you're decreasing your debt, increase your generosity. Long before marriage, give with open hands. The Bible teaches we should give the first 10 percent to God. (Everything we have is His, anyway.) Then we learn to give beyond the tithe, offering sacrificially to those in need and to worthwhile ministries.

If you develop a lifestyle of stewardship and generosity now, you'll carry God's blessings into your future marriage.

Habit 7. "I Will Invest in My Relationship with God."

In chapter 4, I told you about the season in my life when I determined to date only Jesus. Instead of pursuing the next hot number every weekend, as had been my habit before God changed my heart, I set apart time to study the person and teachings of Jesus and let His Spirit change my desires and emotions.

For my seventh habit of the heart, I recommend that you make a priority of a similar commitment. That's because I've found that dating Jesus is a habit that goes right to the heart of preparing spiritually for marriage.

Does dating Jesus mean that every Friday night, you put on one of your favorite outfits, slap on some lip gloss, and meet Jesus at the theater for the new Will Ferrell flick? I hope not.

What do you do when you're dating an ordinary person? You make that person a priority. You think about her. You desire to please him. You enjoy getting to know her. You spend time with him.

How about doing those things with Jesus? The time you have as an unmarried person—whether it's weeks or years—is a gift. Without the responsibility of a spouse, you can devote yourself without distraction to Jesus. As Paul wrote:

> An unmarried man is concerned about the Lord's affairs—how he can please the Lord. But a married man is concerned about the affairs of this world—how he can please his wife—and his interests are divided. An unmarried woman...is concerned about the Lord's affairs: Her aim is to be devoted to the Lord in both body and spirit. But a married woman is concerned about the affairs of this world—how she can please her husband. (1 Corinthians 7:32–34)

Remember, the more you're like Jesus, the better your future marriage will be. Jesus was a humble, obedient, submitted, self-sacrificing servant. He lived with integrity, boldly defending the truth and the people under His care. If you're growing in those qualities, you're well on your way to giving God's best to someone else!

In practical terms, how can you cultivate that intimate relationship with Jesus? How can you make Him more and more your life priority as you prepare for your life partner?

Spiritual habits differ from person to person. Ask yourself,

What draws me close to God? Is it worship? How about when you pray? Or fast? Does God speak to you when you're serving people? When you're listening to the Bible on your iPod? Make those things an important part of your daily life.

Imagine how boring it would become if you did the same thing on every date. Every Friday at seven you meet at the same restaurant, order the same food, have the same conversation, then go home. *Blah!* If you approach God the same way every time, you'll get the same results. Seek Him creatively. Make Him a part of everything you do. Talk to Him on the commute to work or school. Imagine Him sitting beside you. Ask Him questions. Tell Him stories. Be quiet and listen. When it rains, think about His creation. When someone is aching, pause and ask Him to give you words of comfort. When you're aching and feel all alone, cry with Him.

Since you're sharing your life with Jesus, why not pray daily for your future spouse? You may not have met the person, but God knows whom you'll marry. Pray for him to grow closer to Christ, for God to prepare him, protect her, and reveal Himself to her.

On my many dates with Jesus, I wrote thoughts about what He was teaching me, letters to my future wife, and prayers for her. By the time I met Amy, I had a shoe box full of notes. One day, after we knew we were heading for marriage, I gave her the box. When she realized what it signified, she cried.

God had laid the foundation for our marriage during those divine dates.

Becoming the Two of Someone Else's Dreams

Having officiated well over three hundred weddings, I've seen a lot of great relationships start. And unfortunately, I've seen some that never had a chance.

From the perspective of a person in the pew, most weddings appear very similar. The bride's and groom's families typically make the occasion as nice as their budgets allow. All the special people are present, including college friends, childhood friends, co-workers, extended family, even Uncle Odvaar from Oslo. (He's the uncle with the really bad breath and the creepy comb-over.)

At the right moment, the wedding song starts; the bride walks in; the groom shifts his weight, simultaneously nervous and excited; and the mother of the bride grins from ear to ear clutching a small paper-mill's worth of wadded tissue in one hand. In the reception area, there'll be a cake, some punch, and plenty of towels, toasters, and table settings nicely wrapped in white.

From the outside, it all looks pretty much the same from one wedding to the next.

It's what's inside of the couple that makes—or breaks—a marriage.

As I prepare to lead a couple in their vows, I always pray. Sometimes it's a prayer of desperation: *God, please help them. Give me some words to say that might point them in the right direction.* Deep down, I wonder if they know what they're about to do. Truthfully, they often don't.

Instead of preparing their hearts for a lifelong commitment, they simply prepared a wedding.

Other times, my prayer is a prayer of thanksgiving: *God, I praise You for what You have done in their lives. Even more so, I thank You for what You are going to do.*

Some couples stand at the altar prepared to give their best to God and each other. Because they spent time getting ready to be someone's Two before they ever met.

As God is preparing someone else for you, He wants to prepare you for that other person. Ask God to help you *become* your future spouse's right person. And when you are, you will be the answer to someone else's prayers.

15

A COVENANT FOR LIFE

Twenty-two-year-old Tommy signed the back of his high school graduation picture as a gift to his girlfriend, Mandy.

"Dearest Mandy..." His tongue protruded as he used his best handwriting. "You're the love of my life. I promise to love you always. Yours forever, Tommy."

At the bottom he scrawled a P.S.: "If we ever break up, I want this picture back."

A promise today doesn't mean much, does it? If you're a Christ follower, it should. The New Testament teaches us to make sure that our "yes" means yes, and our "no" means no (see James 5:12). Our promises should be forever.

I'm guessing you've heard plenty of marriage vows. You

know, the "I promise to love, honor, and cherish...until death do us part."

The problem with most wedding promises is that what we really mean is, "I will...but only if you will." Between the "love, honor, and cherish" and the "until" comes a truckload of conditions.

Sealing the Deal...Sort Of

The conditions are perfectly reasonable, of course. But a promise built on conditions is actually more like a contract—a business agreement that only stays in effect as long as both parties deliver according to the fine print.

When I owned rental homes, I always had the tenants sign a contract. Why? I was covering my backside. If they didn't do what they said, I could kick them out or garnish their check.

Instead of surrendering my rights and increasing responsibility, a contract seeks to do the opposite. The goal of a smart contract is to increase my rights while decreasing my responsibility. Any businessperson will tell you that a carefully thought-out and detailed contract makes total sense. You don't want to leave anything to chance. And the more that's at stake, the more chances people and circumstances can let you down.

But in marriage, a contract only helps in court. *It doesn't help in your relationship at all.* In fact, contracts and the mindset that goes with them only lead to trouble.

I want to close this book on finding and keeping a marriage that goes the distance with a very radical idea:

Don't build your marriage on a contract.

Build it on a covenant.

Bound by Love and Blood

Covenant isn't used much in normal conversation these days. So what is it exactly? It's an unconditional, binding agreement between two parties before God. It comes from the Hebrew word *beriyth* (ber-EET) and literally means "cutting."

In the Old Testament, two parties often sealed their covenant agreement with a profoundly symbolic ceremony. One person would kill a bull or some other animal and *cut* the animal in half. (This is no bull.) Then he'd walk between the halves, promising the other person, "If I break my covenant vow with you, may God do to me what I've done to this animal." That's a serious commitment.

So is the covenant bond of marriage.

Think of a marriage covenant as an unconditional surrendering of one's rights while increasing one's responsibility. When I married Amy, it was unconditional—till death do us part. At the same time, I gave up many rights. I can't do whatever I want anymore. While I willingly let go of previous rights, I gained significant responsibility—to lead, love, and protect my family. Amy did the same. She gave up a lot and picked up a lot of responsibilities—no strings attached.

A covenant is serious business. That's why when an Old Testament couple stood before a priest to make their covenant vows, it wasn't uncommon for the priest to cut the groom's hand with a sharp blade until blood flowed freely. Then he would do the same to the bride. To establish the marriage covenant, the priest would join the two hands and mix the blood, showing that two had become one.

Then, to seal the agreement, the priest would bind their hands with a cord. From that moment on, all that the husband had and all that he was belonged to his wife. All that the wife had and all that she was belonged to her husband.

Thankfully we're under the New Covenant, sealed with the lifeblood of Jesus. (You're probably sighing with relief. No knife will be necessary at your wedding. No mess on your dress.) Today, we create a marriage covenant with vows. In a Christian marriage ceremony, the bride and groom promise before the pastor, witnesses, and God to become partners in Christ. They're still two individuals. But from now on, they have also become something else, something more.

They have become...one.

And the two, we read in Genesis 2:24, *"will become one flesh."*

Two at the Altar

"But how could I enter a covenant?" you might be asking. "It sounds way too risky."

And that's what *Going All the Way* has been about. In these pages, the answer to your concern is, "Yes, it certainly is too risky...unless you choose to prepare for and enter marriage differently—the oddly godly way, the way that God created you for."

On the day of your wedding, you'll stand before your pastor at the altar. In the Bible, an altar was always a place of sacrifice. On that special day, you'll make a sacrifice. And the sacrifice will be...you.

You will die to yourself, join your heart with another, and create a covenant partnership in Christ.

Then you will set out on your journey together with passion and confidence, prepared to receive one of the sweetest gifts two lovers ever hoped might—just might—be true: a marriage that goes all the way—in love, intimacy, purpose, friendship, fulfillment, and years.

ACKNOWLEDGMENTS

To all my friends who offered encouragement and support during the process of writing *Going All the Way,* I am deeply grateful.

I'm especially indebted to:

Brian Smith—you're brilliant. Thanks for pouring your heart into another project. Working with you is a blast. Your contribution was huge—again. Most of all, thanks for your friendship.

David Kopp, Adrienne Spain, and Jennifer Barrow—you contributed so much. Thank you for generously offering your valuable expertise.

Brannon Golden, Aaron Ball, Ginger Ward, Jessica Thayer, Karrie Hraban, and Sarah McLean—thank you for reading the manuscript and offering your insight. Your creative suggestions made a big difference.

Jimmy Evans and Louie Giglio—thank you for your awesome ministries. Your teaching has greatly influenced my life and the ideas in this book.

LifeChurch.tv—thank you for your undying commitment to become fully devoted followers of Christ. Amy and I are thrilled to serve Christ with you for the rest of our lives.

Mom and Dad—thank you for teaching me that with God's help, I could do *anything.*

Catie, Mandy, Anna, Sam, Bookie, and Jo Jo—you are the best kids in the world.

Amy—thank you for our six kids, your unswerving loyalty, and unconditional support. You are the love of my life, my best friend, and a great kisser.

Is the **REAL** you getting lost because the **FAKE** you is just so annoyingly impressive?

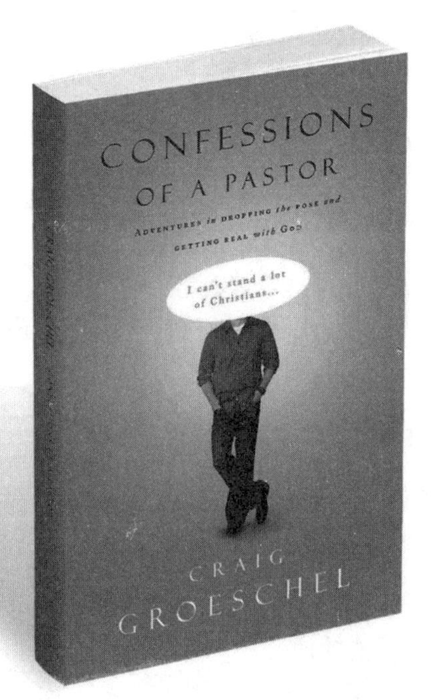

Why do we fake it so much? Why do we spend so much time trying to please everyone else and make so little effort trying to please God? When Craig Groeschel asked himself those questions, he couldn't come up with a good answer. So one day he decided to drop the act and start getting real. With that one choice, his life began to change in a big way. And yours can, too. Craig's passionate, funny, warts-and-all confessions and the lessons he learned from them will help you find your own path to authentic living and a deeper relationship with God (you know He's on to you anyway!).

BOCA RATON PUBLIC LIBRARY, FLORIDA
3 3656 0451738 4